The Complete Guide to
Killer Creatures

The Complete Guide to
Killer Creatures

Jinny Johnson

Contents

A New Burlington Book
Conceived, edited, and designed by Marshall Editions
The Old Brewery
6 Blundell Street
London N7 9BH, UK
www.marshalleditions.com

Managing Editor Paul Docherty
Art Director Ivo Marloh
Design Tim Scrivens
Editorial Elise See Tai
Maps Tim and Ali Scrivens
Production Nikki Ingram

ISBN 10: 1-84566-330-6
ISBN 13: 978-1-84566-330-8

Originated in Hong Kong by Modern Age.
Printed and bound in Singapore by
Star Standard Industries (Pte) Ltd.

10 9 8 7 6 5 4 3 2 1

This page A Namaqua chameleon basks on a sand dune in the Namib Desert of Namibia, Africa; its prey includes insects, lizards, scorpions, and snakes.
Previous pages A Nile crocodile in Botswana, Africa, displays its long jaws and sharp teeth; A brown bear carries its catch of salmon in Kamchatka, Russia.

Introduction to killer creatures

Creatures from every major animal group are included in these pages. They range from tiny insects to huge whales but what they all have in common is that they are hunters—they catch other living creatures to eat.

All animals have to eat some kind of food to provide their bodies with fuel for life. Some feed only on plants. Others eat the plant-eaters—or each other. For the system to work, there must always be many more prey animals than predators.

If we all ate exactly the same food, there would not be enough to go around and lots of other food would go to waste. Fortunately, in the animal kingdom there is something that eats almost every type of food, however strange. Some birds and lizards eat scorpions; there is a wolf spider that can feed on the deadly cane toad; and the kingsnake eats poisonous rattlesnakes. Vultures and beetles feed on animals that have died of natural causes or have been left by other predators.

It is important to remember that animals do not kill out of cruelty. They kill to survive and to feed their young—this is the natural order of life on Earth.

How to use this book

The creatures in these pages are arranged in chapters that correspond to the main groups of animals: mammals, birds, reptiles, amphibians, fish, and insects and other invertebrates. Families or closely related species appear on the same double-page spread. Individual entries are headed by the most generally accepted version of the animal's common name.

Emerald tree boa

The fastest moving of all the boas, the emerald tree boa is an expert climber and also swims well. It has a prehensile tail, which it uses to hold on to branches as it reaches forward to grab prey.

Family	Boidae
Latin name	*Corallus caninus*
Length	5–6½ ft (1.5–2 m)
Distribution	Northern South America

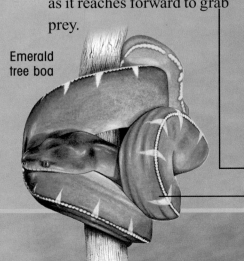

Emerald tree boa

A world map provides a visual summary of the distribution information.

Text and illustrations clearly describe each individual species.

For mammals, birds, reptiles, amphibians, and fish, the name of the family to which the animal belongs is given in each case, as well as its Latin or scientific name. The Latin name remains the same in every country, whatever the language. For some of the insects and invertebrates, the name of the family is given with the number of species in that family. Where applicable, the genus or Latin species name is supplied instead of the number of species in the family.

The approximate size of each animal is also provided along with its distribution. For most creatures, the measurement given is the total length, but for mammals, the head and body length and the tail length are listed separately, with the maximum figure given in each case.

Above This ladybug is feeding on a group of tiny aphids on a plant.
Left This powerful predator, the Bengal tiger, reveals the huge canine teeth in its strong jaws.

Animal classification

At least 1.5 million animal species are known and there may be millions more to be found. Scientists divide the animal kingdom into groups. A brown bear, for instance, is a *species* of bear—a species is a group of similar organisms that can breed together. Bears belong to the bear *family*, which belongs to the *order* of carnivores, in the *class* of mammals. Mammals are part of the *phylum* called *chordates*, which includes all vertebrate animals, as well as some primitive chordates called sea squirts. This chart shows the main animal groups, most of which include some predatory creatures.

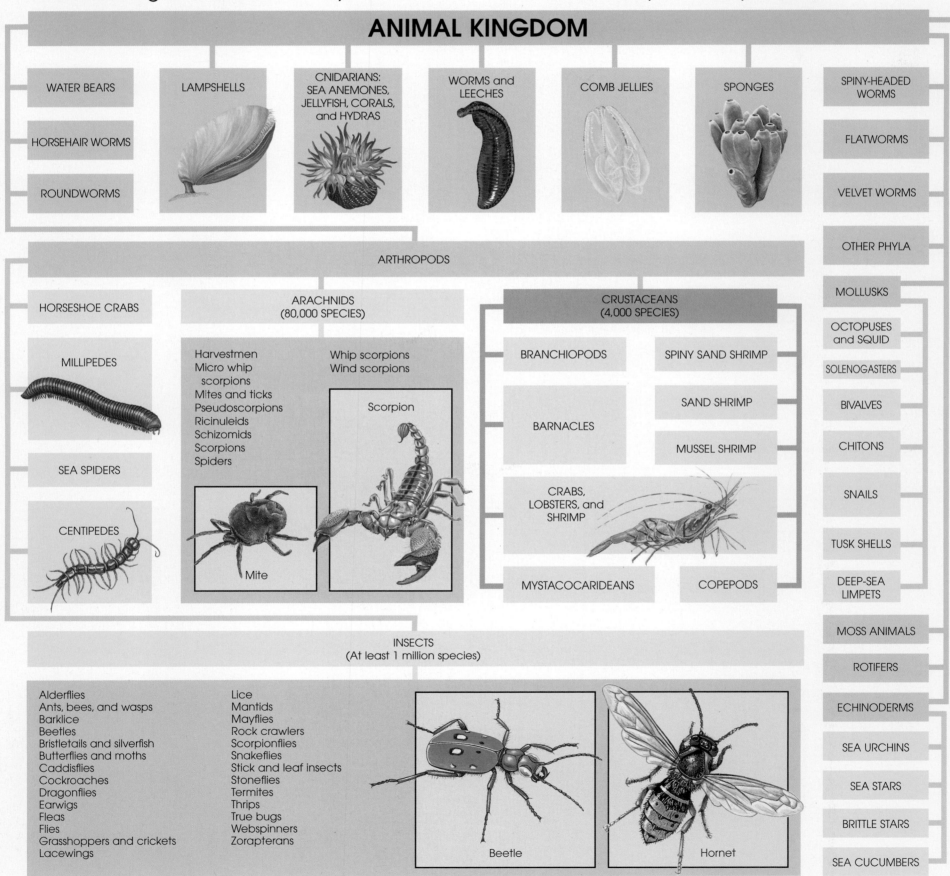

ANIMAL KINGDOM

WATER BEARS

HORSEHAIR WORMS

ROUNDWORMS

LAMPSHELLS

CNIDARIANS:
SEA ANEMONES,
JELLYFISH, CORALS,
and HYDRAS

WORMS and
LEECHES

COMB JELLIES

SPONGES

SPINY-HEADED
WORMS

FLATWORMS

VELVET WORMS

OTHER PHYLA

ARTHROPODS

HORSESHOE CRABS

MILLIPEDES

SEA SPIDERS

CENTIPEDES

ARACHNIDS
(80,000 SPECIES)

Harvestmen
Micro whip
  scorpions
Mites and ticks
Pseudoscorpions
Ricinuleids
Schizomids
Scorpions
Spiders

Whip scorpions
Wind scorpions

Scorpion

Mite

CRUSTACEANS
(4,000 SPECIES)

BRANCHIOPODS

BARNACLES

CRABS,
LOBSTERS, and
SHRIMP

MYSTACOCARIDEANS

SPINY SAND SHRIMP

SAND SHRIMP

MUSSEL SHRIMP

COPEPODS

MOLLUSKS

OCTOPUSES
and SQUID

SOLENOGASTERS

BIVALVES

CHITONS

SNAILS

TUSK SHELLS

DEEP-SEA
LIMPETS

MOSS ANIMALS

ROTIFERS

ECHINODERMS

SEA URCHINS

SEA STARS

BRITTLE STARS

SEA CUCUMBERS

INSECTS
(At least 1 million species)

Alderflies
Ants, bees, and wasps
Barklice
Beetles
Bristletails and silverfish
Butterflies and moths
Caddisflies
Cockroaches
Dragonflies
Earwigs
Fleas
Flies
Grasshoppers and crickets
Lacewings

Lice
Mantids
Mayflies
Rock crawlers
Scorpionflies
Snakeflies
Stick and leaf insects
Stoneflies
Termites
Thrips
True bugs
Webspinners
Zorapterans

Beetle

Hornet

CHORDATES

REPTILES
(8,734 species)

Crocodiles and alligators
Lizards and snakes

Tuataras
Turtles, tortoises, and terrapins

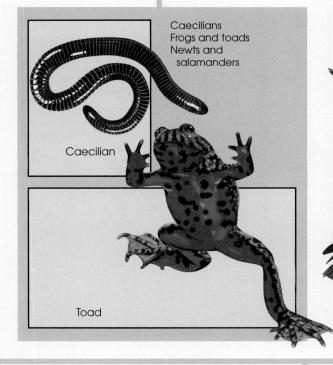

Snake

Crocodile

MAMMALS
(4,475 species)

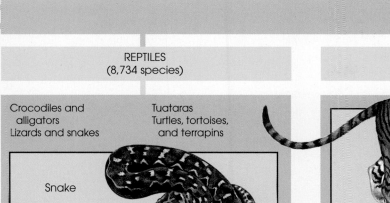

Tiger

Odd-toed hoofed mammals
Pangolins
Primates
Rodents
Seals, sea lions, and walruses
Sea cows
Tree shrews
Whales and dolphins

Aardvarks
Anteaters and relatives
Bats
Carnivores (cats, dogs, and bears)
Dugongs and manatees
Elephants
Elephant shrews

Even-toed hoofed mammals
Flying lemurs
Hares, rabbits, and pikas
Hyraxes
Insectivores
Marsupials (pouched mammals)
Monotremes (egg-laying mammals)

Otter

Hedgehog

AMPHIBIANS
(6,547 species)

Caecilians
Frogs and toads
Newts and salamanders

Caecilian

Toad

BIRDS
(more than 9,000 species)

Gannet

Golden eagle

Albatrosses, petrels, and shearwaters
Birds of prey (eagles, hawks, and vultures)
Cranes, rails, coots, and bustards
Cuckoos and roadrunners
Divers, or loons
Ducks, geese, swans, and screamers
Grebes
Herons, storks, ibises, and flamingos
Kingfishers, bee-eaters, and rollers
Kiwis
Mousebirds
Nightjars and frogmouths
Ostriches
Owls
Parrots
Perching birds, such as robins, rooks, and crows

Pelicans, gannets, cormorants, darters, and frigatebirds
Penguins
Pheasants, jungle fowl, grouse, partridges, turkeys, and quails
Pigeons and doves
Rheas
Sandgrouse
Swifts and hummingbirds
Tinamous
Trogons
Turacos
Wading birds, gulls, terns, and auks
Woodpeckers, barbets, toucans, jacamars, and honeyguides

Penguin

Rook

BONY FISH
(23,500 species)

There are 46 orders including:
Catfish
Cod
Dragonfish

Eels
Flatfish
Lanternfish
Salmon and trout
Perchlike fish

Cod

SHARKS, SKATES, and RAYS
(about 850 species)

Includes nine shark orders and four orders of rays

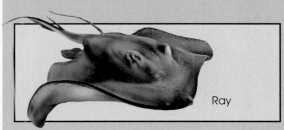

Ray

JAWLESS FISH (88 species)

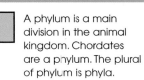

SEA SQUIRTS (about 2,000 species)

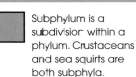

KEY TO THE MAIN ANIMAL GROUPS

A kingdom is the largest grouping of animals. Plants, fungi, protists, and monerans belong to separate kingdoms.

A phylum is a main division in the animal kingdom. Chordates are a phylum. The plural of phylum is phyla.

Subphylum is a subdivision within a phylum. Crustaceans and sea squirts are both subphyla.

A class is a division of a phylum. Reptiles, birds, amphibians, fish, and mammals are classes.

An order is a division of a class of animals. Bats, rodents, marsupials, and primates are orders of mammals.

Mammals

Mammals are warm-blooded vertebrate animals—a vertebrate is an animal with a backbone. There are around 4,475 species of mammals living all over the world and in every kind of habitat. Most mammals live on land, but whales, seals, and dolphins have become adapted to life in water. And mammals in the form of bats have even taken to life in the air.

Life as a hunter

The top mammal predators, such as tigers and wolves, have highly efficient weapons in the form of sharp teeth and claws. They are also strong, highly intelligent, and have very well developed senses. Some, such as cheetahs and tigers, hunt alone. Others, including hunting dogs and wolves, prefer to live and hunt in packs.

The young of most predatory mammals are born naked, blind, and helpless. They are completely dependent on their parents for the first stage of their lives. There is a lot to learn, and the young of such expert predators as big cats and dogs must be taught their skills by their parents in order to survive as adults. Big cats, for example, spend at least a year with their mother, learning how to find, track, and kill prey. And when young mammals pounce and wrestle with one another, they are actually practicing their hunting and fighting techniques for the future when they will have to live and hunt on their own.

Left Lions often hunt in groups, but these cats are always on the watch for prey and will kill alone if the opportunity arises.

Bandicoots and quolls

All of these animals are carnivorous marsupials, which live in Australia or Tasmania. They are active, intelligent predators and are adapted to hunt down the prey they need to survive. The dasyurid family includes about 62 species, ranging in size from tiny mouse-sized animals to the large Tasmanian devil. There are about 21 species of bandicoots and only one numbat.

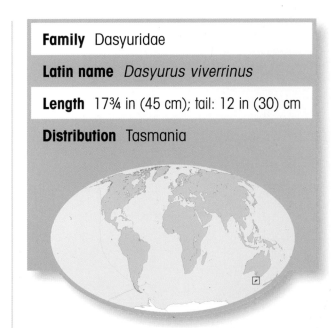

Family	Dasyuridae
Latin name	*Dasyurus viverrinus*
Length	17¾ in (45 cm); tail: 12 in (30) cm
Distribution	Tasmania

Tasmanian devil

Quoll

Tasmanian devil

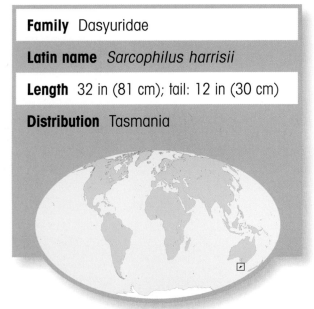

Family	Dasyuridae
Latin name	*Sarcophilus harrisii*
Length	32 in (81 cm); tail: 12 in (30 cm)
Distribution	Tasmania

The Tasmanian devil, the largest carnivorous marsupial, has very strong jaws and can crunch through the bones of its prey. It preys on anything it comes across, from insects and small creatures to sheep. It will also feed on carrion—animals that are already dead. Normally active at night, it makes a loud screeching noise if alarmed.

Quoll

The cat-sized quoll is a fierce little predator with a pointed snout and sharp teeth. It hunts rats, rabbits, and invertebrate animals, usually at night, and also eats fruit and carrion—animals that are already dead. Quolls used to be shot by farmers for killing chickens, but now it is realised that they do more good than harm by killing pests. During the day, the quoll shelters among rocks or in a hollow log.

Eastern barred bandicoot

This aggressive marsupial shelters in a nest on the ground during the day and comes out at night to prey on worms and other creatures. It tears into the ground with its sharp claws and then probes for prey with its nose.

Family	Peramelidae
Latin name	*Perameles gunnii*
Length	14 in (35.5 cm); tail: 4¼ in (11 cm)
Distribution	Southeast Australia, Tasmania

Eastern barred bandicoot

Mulgara

Family	Dasyuridae
Latin name	*Dasycercus cristicauda*
Length	8½ in (21.5 cm); tail: 5 in (13 cm)
Distribution	West and central Australia

The mulgara is perfectly adapted for life as a desert predator. During the heat of the day, it hides in a burrow and then emerges at night to gobble up insects as well as lizards, mice, and baby snakes. It never drinks and gets all the liquid it needs from its prey.

Mulgara

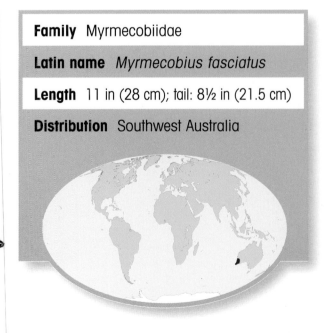

Numbat

The numbat feeds almost entirely on termites, gobbling up as many as 20,000 a day. It tears open termite nests with its long clawed feet and then sweeps the insects into its mouth with its long sticky tongue. Its teeth are tiny but it has 52 of them, more than any other land mammal.

Family	Myrmecobiidae
Latin name	*Myrmecobius fasciatus*
Length	11 in (28 cm); tail: 8½ in (21.5 cm)
Distribution	Southwest Australia

Numbat

Moles and shrews

These creatures are all insectivores, a group of mammals that includes moles, hedgehogs, shrews, and moonrats among other creatures. A typical insectivore has a long, very mobile snout and is most active at night when it roots around for small prey. Most have tiny eyes and small ears, but for many of these animals, smell is the most important sense for finding prey.

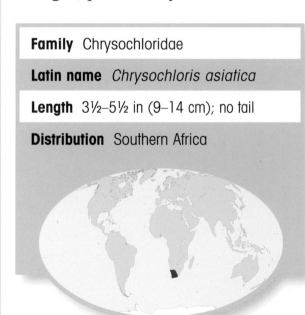

Cape golden mole

Cape golden mole

This mole has strong claws on its front feet, which help it burrow underground. It hunts small creatures, such as beetles and worms, as it burrows but may also root around on the ground's surface at night, particularly after rain.

Family	Chrysochloridae
Latin name	*Chrysochloris asiatica*
Length	3½–5½ in (9–14 cm); no tail
Distribution	Southern Africa

Moonrat

This long-snouted creature hunts at night for insects and worms and will also plunge into freshwater and swim in search of fish and crabs. It lives alone and marks its territory with a strong-smelling secretion from glands near its tail. This foul smell puts off all but the most determined enemies.

Family	Erinaceidae
Latin name	*Echinosorex gymnura*
Length	18 in (46 cm); tail: 12 in (30 cm)
Distribution	Southeast Asia

Moonrat

Desert hedgehog

Family	Erinaceidae
Latin name	*Paraechinus aethiopicus*
Length	9 in (23 cm); tail: 1½ in (4 cm)
Distribution	North Africa, Middle East

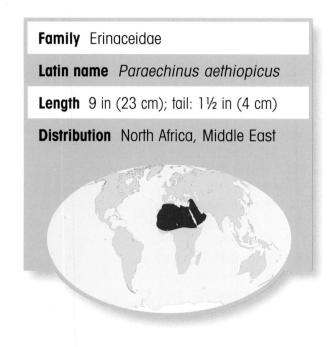

The desert hedgehog has found a way to eat scorpions—it nips off the stings before swallowing them. It also preys on other invertebrate animals, which it snaps up with its slender jaws, and it eats birds' eggs. It rarely needs to drink and gets most of the water it needs from its prey.

Desert hedgehog

Masked shrew

This little creature is always on the move, day and night, and has a long slender snout that constantly twitches as it searches for prey to eat. It darts over the ground or burrows into the soil as it hunts for worms, snails, and other small creatures.

Family	Soricidae
Latin name	*Sorex cinereus*
Length	3¾ in (9.5 cm); tail: 3 in (8 cm)
Distribution	Northern North America

Masked shrew

Cuban solenodon

Family	Solenodontidae
Latin name	*Solenodon cubanus*
Length	12½ in (32 cm); tail: 10 in (25 cm)
Distribution	Cuba

This shrewlike creature is a fast mover and can also climb into the lower branches of trees. It hunts for food, such as insects and other small creatures, by tearing into rotting logs with its strong claws or probing the ground with its long snout. The solenodon also has a poisonous bite and can use this to stun larger prey, such as lizards and rodents. It is not immune to its own poison and rival males sometimes kill each other when fighting.

Cuban solenodon

Bats

There are mammals that can glide from tree to tree, but bats are the only mammals that can truly fly. Some bats eat only fruit and other plant food, but many are predators that hunt insects and sometimes larger creatures, such as fish. Bats use echolocation to help them find flying prey at night. The bat makes a series of clicking sounds and the echoes of these tell the bat the size and position of any nearby prey.

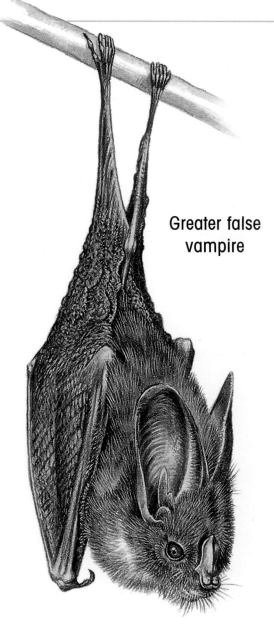

Greater false vampire

Family	Phyllostomidae
Latin name	*Desmodus rotundus*
Length	3½ in (9 cm); tail: 2½ in (6 cm)
Distribution	Central and South America

Vampire bat

Strictly speaking, this bat is not a predator, as it does not kill its victim. It feeds only on blood. At night, the bat searches out warm-blooded prey, such as a cow or horse, crawls up onto it and shaves away a small piece of flesh. It then laps up the blood—a special ingredient in the bat's saliva prevents the blood from clotting while the bat feeds.

Greater false vampire

This is a very carnivorous bat—it regularly catches rodents, frogs, fish, and even other bats as well as insects and spiders. It generally carries its prey back to its roosting site to eat and piles of bones may gather on the ground below.

Family	Megadermatidae
Latin name	*Megaderma lyra*
Length	2½–3¼ in (6–8 cm); no tail
Distribution	South Asia and parts of Southeast Asia

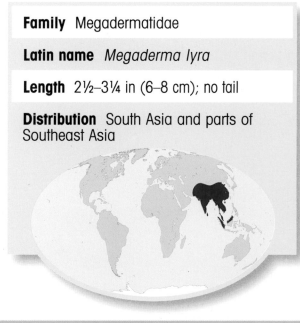

Vampire bat

Big brown bat

This fast-flying bat is very common all over its range. It preys mostly on beetles as well as wasps and ants, but rarely eats moths or flies.

It is a popular bat with farmers as it also feeds on a number of bugs that cause damage to their crops.

Big brown bat

Family Vespertilionidae

Latin name *Eptesicus fuscus*

Length 3 in (8 cm); tail: 2 in (5 cm)

Distribution North America, Caribbean islands

Family Megadermatidae

Latin name *Cardioderma cor*

Length 3 in (8 cm); no tail

Distribution East and central Africa

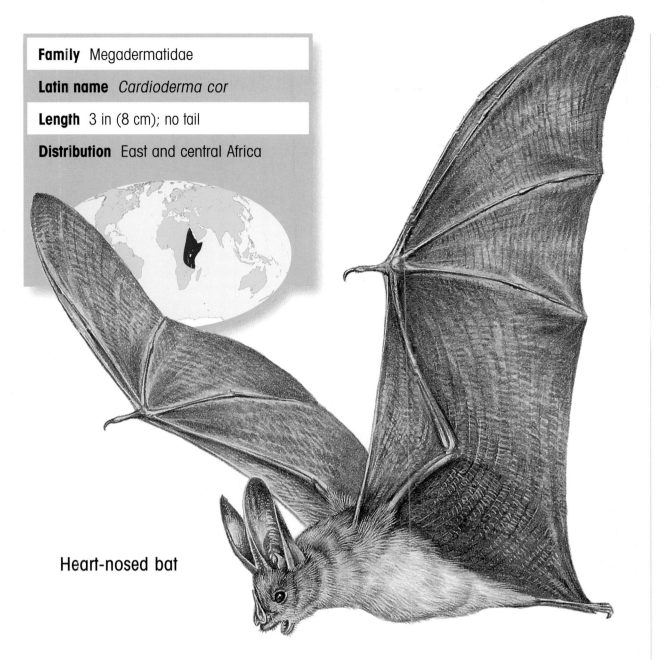

Heart-nosed bat

Heart-nosed bat

This bat feeds on lizards as well as insects and will also catch other bats. It attacks the bats in flight, and hits them with its powerful wings to disrupt their flight. This bat is a strong flier and can take off from the ground while carrying prey as big as itself.

Philippine horseshoe bat

Large, slow-flying insects and heavily armored ground beetles are the main prey of this bat. Its teeth are very sharp and it can slice through the insects' thick wing cases before eating them.

Family Rhinolophidae

Latin name *Rhinolophus philippinensis*

Length 3½ in (9 cm); tail: 1 in (2.5 cm)

Distribution Philippine Islands

Philippine horseshoe bat

Rats and other rodents

Rodents are among the most common of all mammals. They are very adaptable and able to survive in many different conditions and eat almost any kind of food. Many rodents feed mostly on plants and grain, but some are efficient predators that will attack almost anything that comes their way.

Family	Muridae
Latin name	*Hydromys chrysogaster*
Length	15½ in (39 cm); tail: 13 in (33 cm)
Distribution	New Guinea, Australia

Australian water rat

This large sleek rat is the largest rodent in Australia. Much of its time is spent in water and it is well adapted for hunting aquatic prey. It has webbed back feet for swimming, thick waterproof fur, and nostrils and eyes set high on its head. It is a powerful predator and is able to seize fish as well as frogs, shellfish, and waterbirds in its large teeth.

Brown rat

Brown rat

The brown rat is one of the most successful and widespread of all mammals and lives alongside humans all over the world. Fast, agile, and intelligent, the rat will eat almost anything it comes across but it does seem to like meat. It catches birds, eats their eggs, is expert at catching fish, and kills other rodents, such as mice. Working in packs, it can kill creatures much larger than itself, including young lambs and pigs. Rats have also been known to attack young humans.

Family	Muridae
Latin name	*Rattus norvegicus*
Length	11 in (28 cm); tail: 9 in (23 cm)
Distribution	Worldwide, except polar regions

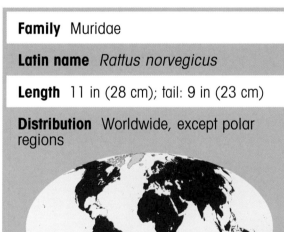

Australian water rat

Family	Myoxidae
Latin name	*Myoxus glis*
Length	8 in (20 cm); tail: 7 in (18 cm)
Distribution	Central and southern Europe, western Asia

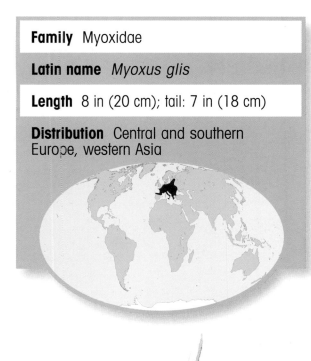

Edible dormouse

Northern grasshopper mouse

Grasshoppers and scorpions are the main prey of this very predatory little mouse, and it will also hunt other mice. It usually stalks its prey, then pounces and kills with a bite to the head. If catching scorpions, the mouse starts by biting off the stinging tail. With grasshoppers, it goes for the jumping legs so its victims cannot escape.

Family	Muridae
Latin name	*Onychomys leucogaster*
Length	5 in (13 cm); tail: 2¼ in (6 cm)
Distribution	Western North America

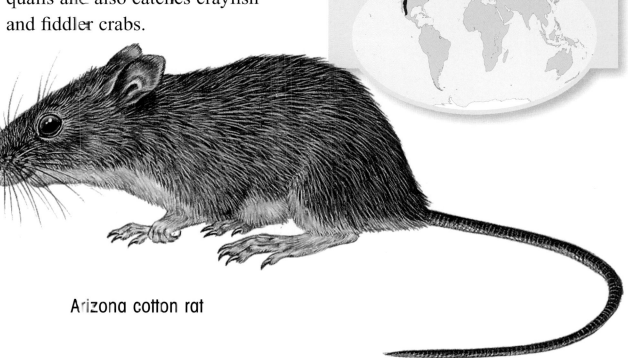

Northern grasshopper mouse

Arizona cotton rat

This sturdy rat sometimes occurs in huge numbers. It normally feeds on seeds and insects, but when numbers are very high it steals the eggs and young of birds, such as quails and also catches crayfish and fiddler crabs.

Family	Muridae
Latin name	*Sigmodon arizonae*
Length	8 in (20 cm); tail: 5 in (13 cm)
Distribution	Southwest North America

Edible dormouse

As an excellent climber, the dormouse scurries through the trees at night searching for food. It does eat some plant food, such as seeds and nuts, but also catches insects and even young birds. During the summer, it eats as much as possible so it can put on plenty of fat to keep it going through its winter hibernation. This species is the largest of the dormice.

Arizona cotton rat

Wolves and foxes

These animals all belong to the dog family and are strong, muscular, fast-running predators. They hunt by chasing their prey or by stalking, then pouncing. All have long sharp teeth at the front of the jaw for stabbing prey and larger teeth farther back for slicing flesh and crushing bones.

Arctic fox

Lemmings are a favorite prey of the Arctic fox, but it catches other small rodents and birds or any other creatures it comes across, too. It also follows polar bears to take any leftovers from their kills, and will dig down into the snow to reach the pups of ringed seals in their den.

Family	Canidae
Latin name	*Vulpes zerda*
Length	16 in (41 cm); tail: 12 in (30 cm)
Distribution	North Africa to the Middle East

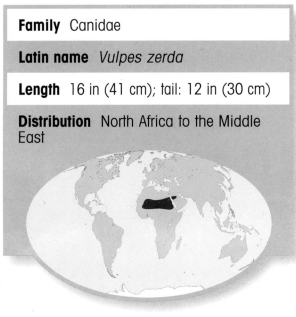

Fennec fox

The fennec, the smallest of the foxes, spends the heat of the day in an underground den and comes out at night to prey on rodents, birds, insects, and lizards. It is a good digger and often digs up burrowing creatures.

Arctic fox

Fennec fox

Family	Canidae
Latin name	*Alopex lagopus*
Length	6 in (66 cm); tail: 16½ in (42 cm)
Distribution	Arctic regions of Europe, Asia and North America

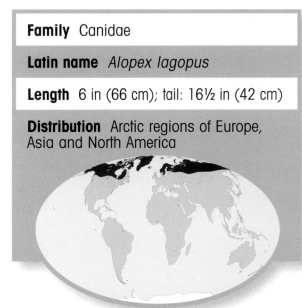

Red fox

An intelligent, adaptable animal, the red fox can live in many different kinds of habitats and has proved very successful at coping with life in towns and cities. It is a skillful hunter, and preys on animals, such as rats, mice, rabbits, and birds, but is also a scavenger and will take any waste food it can find. It generally lives alone, except in the breeding season when the male finds food for his mate and cubs.

Red fox

Family	Canidae
Latin name	*Vulpes vulpes*
Length	35 in (89 cm); tail: 20 in (51 cm)
Distribution	North America, Europe, Asia, North Africa, Australia

Coyote

Coyote

The coyote generally hunts alone, stalking and pouncing on small animals. But when hunting larger prey, coyotes may work together to chase and bring down their victim. The coyote has also been known to hunt with a badger. It sniffs out rodents in their underground burrow and the badger then digs them up with its claws.

Family	Canidae
Latin name	*Canis latrans*
Length	38 in (96.5 cm); tail: 15 in (38 cm)
Distribution	North and Central America

Gray wolf

Family	Canidae
Latin name	*Canis lupus*
Length	5 ft (1.5 m); tail: 20 in (51 cm)
Distribution	North America, parts of Europe, Asia

Gray wolf

The gray wolf is the largest of the dog family—it hunts in packs of a dozen or so animals and can bring down animals as large as moose, caribou, and musk oxen as well as smaller creatures, such as rodents. Wolves hunt by following a scent trail, then stalking the prey until as close as possible before starting the final chase. The hunters share the kill with the rest of the pack.

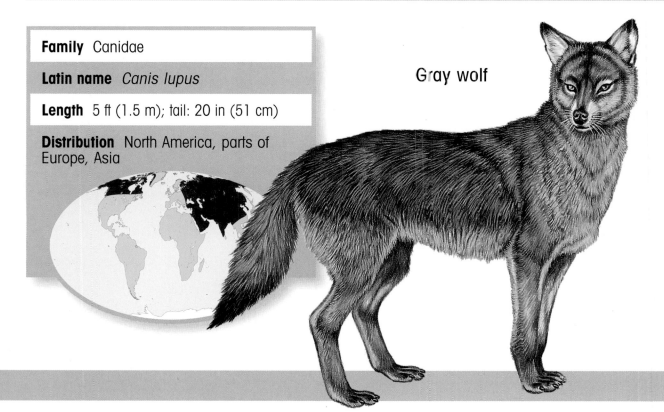

Jackals and dogs

All members of the dog family have well-developed senses, but the sense of smell is the most important for hunting. Dogs rely on smell for tracking their prey as well as for picking up scent messages about other animals in their area. A dog can pick up odors in concentrations about 100 million times lower than a person can. Dogs also have excellent hearing and good eyesight.

Family	Canidae
Latin name	*Canis dingo*
Length	43 in (109 cm); tail: 14 in (35.5 cm)
Distribution	Australia

Dingo

Black-backed jackal

Family	Canidae
Latin name	*Canis mesomelas*
Length	35 in (90 cm); tail: 16 in (41 cm)
Distribution	East and southern Africa

Jackals are known as scavengers, but they also hunt and kill their own food. Small animals, such as hares and rats, are their main prey, but jackals can also bring down small antelopes. Jackals that live on the coast of Namibia go to seal breeding beaches and prey on newborn seal pups.

Dingo

The dingo may be a descendent of the domestic dog, but it now lives wild over much of Australia. These dogs prey on animals, such as kangaroos, wallabies, and rabbits, but they also kill sheep so are regarded as pests by farmers. Dingoes live in family groups and sometimes hunt in packs so they can bring down large prey. Young male dingoes generally move around and hunt alone.

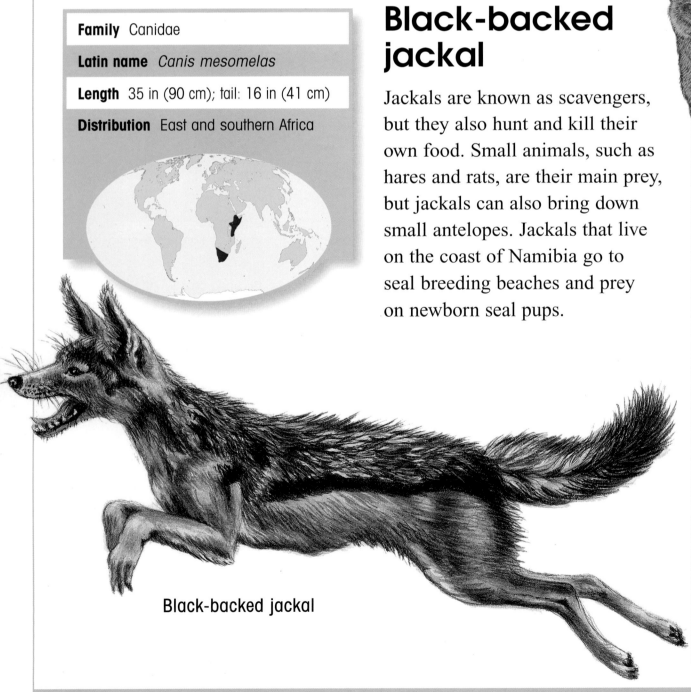

Black-backed jackal

Bush dog

Family	Canidae
Latin name	*Speothos venaticus*
Length	30 in (76 cm); tail: 6 in (15 cm)
Distribution	Northern South America

The bush dog lives and hunts in packs of up to ten animals. Large rodents, such as pacas and agoutis, are its main prey, and the bush dog will chase animals into water. This animal has shorter legs than most of its relatives and also has the shortest tail and fewest teeth (only 38) of any dog.

Bush dog

Dhole

The dhole hunts in packs, usually taking down animals much larger than itself, such as water buffalo and deer. It tracks its prey by scent and then starts the chase. Although the dhole is not a particularly fast runner, it can keep going for long distances, pursuing its victim until the animal is exhausted. The pack may also split up, one dog moving to cut off the victim's escape route while others surround it. Once the prey is down, the dogs disembowel it—they remove the victim's bowels— and then start to feed. Like all dogs, the dhole has strong, sharp teeth for tearing its prey apart.

Family	Canidae
Latin name	*Cuon alpinus*
Length	44½ in (113 cm); tail: 20 in (51 cm)
Distribution	South and Southeast Asia

Dhole

Raccoon dog

This dog usually lives near water and is a good swimmer. Unusually for a dog, it also climbs well. It eats a wide variety of food from frogs, crabs, and fish to rats, mice, and birds and also scavenges around human settlements for food waste. Although the raccoon dog generally hunts alone it does sometimes gather in a group of 5 or 6 dogs to chase after larger prey.

Family	Canidae
Latin name	*Nyctereutes procyonoides*
Length	23½ in (60 cm); tail: 7 in (18 cm)
Distribution	Parts of Europe and central and eastern Asia

Raccoon dog

Hunting in packs

Creatures from ants to lions have discovered that there is great strength in numbers. By gathering together and hunting in groups, predators can tackle and bring down much larger prey than any one animal could manage alone. Hunting together means that animals can share the effort—for example, they can take it in turn to chase prey at high speed. But to be successful, pack hunters must be organized and able to communicate well with each other.

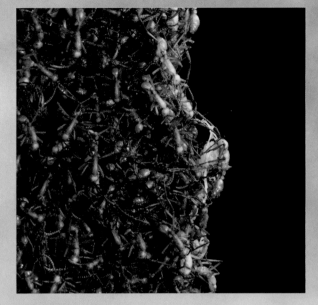

Above Army ants travel in groups of 200,000 or more and swiftly kill much larger insects in their path.

Working together

African hunting dogs specialize in working as a pack. Individually, the dogs are well equipped for killing prey with their sharp teeth and strong jaws. But they are not big animals and could not tackle large prey alone. A pack usually contains up to about 20 animals, led by a dominant male. The pack spends much of the day sleeping or grooming and at dusk, the male leads his pack on a hunt for prey, such as wildebeests, antelopes, or zebras. Once the pack sees a herd of prey, they start to move slowly toward it. Once they are within about 150 ft (45 m), they begin to run at top speed. The dogs may start by chasing different animals, but the pack soon singles out one victim for the kill. When the dogs catch up with their prey, they attack together to bring the animal down. The dogs then share the kill with their young and any other pack members who were not on the hunt.

A predatory pride

Of all the cats, big and small, the lion is the only one that hunts in a group, called a pride. The others all make their kills alone. A lion pride usually includes up to three males, as well as females and their young. The females do most of the hunting and work together to track down and kill large prey, such as zebras and wildebeests. The whole pride then shares the kill. Youngsters join the hunt when they are about a year old.

Above African hunting dogs are intelligent, fast-moving hunters with strong jaws for killing prey, such as this kudu.

Bears

The bears are the largest of all land-living carnivores. As a big, sturdy animal, a typical bear has a bulky head, short legs, and a short tail. The five-toed feet all have large curved claws. Only the polar bear lives entirely on meat. The other seven species have a more mixed diet, but can still be extremely aggressive animals.

American black bear

Polar bear

This huge animal is a surprisingly fast runner and can outrun prey, such as reindeer, over short distances. More often, though, it hunts by stealth—staying well out of sight, it watches for seals coming up for air at breathing holes in the ice. When it spies a seal, the bear moves nearer and then grabs it the next time the seal comes up for air. Using its excellent sense of smell, the bear can sniff out a seal nursery under the snow. It scratches away the top layer of soil and then jumps on to its front feet, pressing down as hard as possible so that the den collapses inward and the unfortunate babies are revealed. It can also swim well and catches prey, such as seals, birds, and even walruses, in the water.

Family	Ursidae
Latin name	*Ursus americanus*
Length	6 ft (1.8 m); tail: 4¾ in (12 cm)
Distribution	North America

Polar bear

Family	Ursidae
Latin name	*Ursus maritimus*
Length	8¼ ft (2.5 m); tail: 5 in (13 cm)
Distribution	Arctic regions around the North Pole

American black bear

The black bear is usually active at night when it roams long distances in search of small mammals and fish as well as fruit, nuts, and honey. It also eats carrion and food waste if it comes across any. Smell is the most important sense for finding its food.

Sun bear

Sun bear

Family	Ursidae
Latin name	*Helarctos malayanus*
Length	4½ ft (1.4 m); tail: 2¾ in (7 cm)
Distribution	Southeast Asia

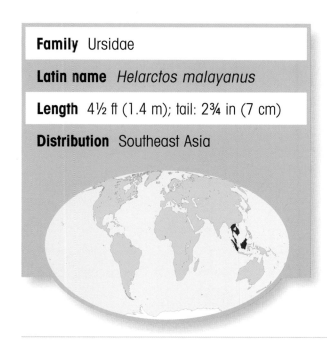

The smallest of the bear family, the sun bear has strong arms with big paws and long curved claws, which it uses to break into the nests of bees and termites. Once the bear has broken into a termite nest, it places one paw inside at a time until it is covered with termites and then licks the insects off. It also preys on rodents and on birds, such as jungle fowl.

Asiatic black bear

This bear is an aggressive predator—it kills cattle, sheep, and goats as well as smaller creatures. Like other bears, it is very strong and can kill a buffalo by breaking its neck.

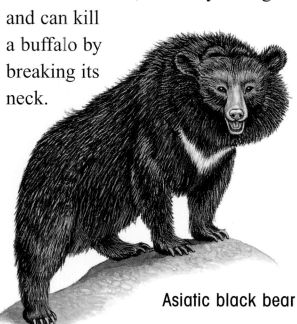

Asiatic black bear

Family	Ursidae
Latin name	*Ursus thibetanus*
Length	6¼ ft (1.9 m); tail: 4 in (10 cm)
Distribution	East, south, and Southeast Asia

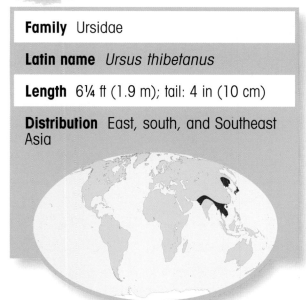

Family	Ursidae
Latin name	*Ursus arctos*
Length	9¾ ft (3 m); tail: 8 in (20 cm)
Distribution	Northern North America and Asia; parts of Europe

Brown bear

This immensely strong creature is the largest of the bears—it feeds on anything that is available, including fruit, nuts, and roots as well as animal prey. In areas where there are salmon rivers, it hooks the fish out of the water with its huge paws as they travel upstream to spawn. Though not a fast runner, it can kill large animals, such as wild boar and moose, particularly if they are old or sick, and its huge canine teeth slice easily through tough flesh.

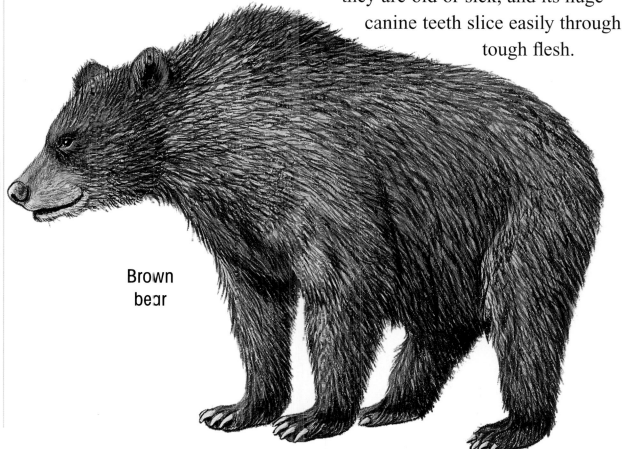

Brown bear

Weasels, ferrets, and polecats

There are about 67 species in this family. Known as the mustelids, the group includes otters and badgers as well as weasels and ferrets. All are expert predators and have sharp teeth and claws for attacking prey. They are found over much of the world, except Australia, Madagascar, and some islands. Weasels and ferrets have been introduced into New Zealand to kill rodents.

Black-footed ferret

This ferret is thought to have become extinct in the wild, but animals bred in captivity have now been successfully reintroduced into some areas. Prairie dogs are the ferret's main prey. It will set up home in a prairie dog tunnel and eat the residents, but it also hunts ground squirrels, rabbits, and birds, and eats carrion. The ferret generally sleeps during the day and goes out to hunt at night.

Family	Mustelidae
Latin name	*Mustela nigripes*
Length	16 in (41 cm); tail: 5 in (13 cm)
Distribution	Central North America

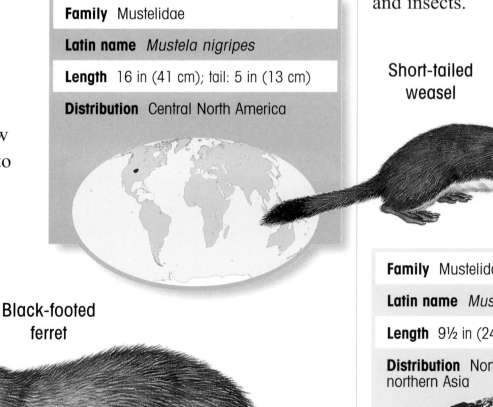

Black-footed ferret

Short-tailed weasel

Also known as the ermine or stoat, this animal is a highly skilled predator and sometimes kills more than it needs and hides it away for another time. Rabbits and rodents are its main prey. It kills by making a powerful and accurate bite on the back of its victim's neck. It also preys on animals larger than itself, such as hares, as well as birds, fish, and insects.

Short-tailed weasel

Family	Mustelidae
Latin name	*Mustela erminea*
Length	9½ in (24 cm); tail: 4¾ in (12 cm)
Distribution	North America, Europe, and northern Asia

European polecat

Family Mustelidae

Latin name *Mustela putorius*

Length 18 in (46 cm); tail: 7½ in (19 cm)

Distribution Europe

Like many of its family, the European polecat takes whatever prey it can find, including rats, mice, frogs, birds, and insects, and kills the creature with a swift bite to the neck. It can also catch animals larger than itself, such as rabbits. The foul-smelling secretions from the scent glands near its tail are used to mark its territory and warn off other polecats.

European polecat

American marten

The marten is an agile and acrobatic predator, and chases squirrels through the trees. Usually, though, it hunts on the ground, catching birds, mice, and other small creatures. It also swims well. Like other mustelids, it holds its prey with its claws and kills by biting into the neck.

Family Mustelidae

Latin name *Martes americana*

Length 17¾ in (45 cm); tail: 9 in (23 cm)

Distribution North America

American marten

Wolverine

One of the biggest of its family, the wolverine is a fierce predator, which can kill prey larger than itself, such as deer and wild sheep. It can run, climb, and swim and is so strong it has even been known to drive cougars away from their kills. The wolverine's jaws are exceptionally strong and it can crush frozen meat and bones.

Family Mustelidae

Latin name *Gulo gulo*

Length 39 in (100 cm); tail: 10¼ in (26 cm)

Distribution Northern North America, Europe, and Asia

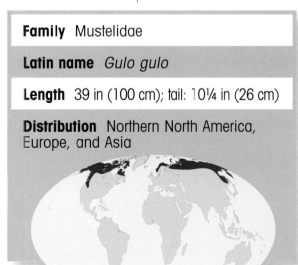

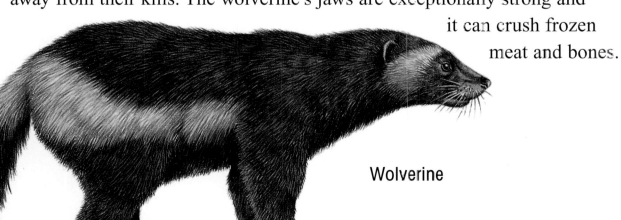

Wolverine

Badgers, skunks, and otters

All of these animals belong to the mustelid family (see p. 28). Like their relatives, they are meat-eaters, although some, such as badgers, also eat plant food. Mustelids hunt mainly by smell but most also have good hearing and sight.

Honey badger

Also known as the ratel, this heavily built badger has a powerful body, short legs, and long claws on its front feet. Bee larvae and honey are its favorite foods and the honey badger has a strange association with a bird called the honeyguide. The bird spies out a bees' nest and leads the badger to it with special calls. The badger then breaks into the nest with its strong claws and shares the food with the bird. The badger's skin is so tough it seems unaffected by the bees' stings. It also hunts small mammals, birds, and reptiles.

Eurasian badger

The badger has a very varied diet and hunts rodents, birds, frogs, and lizards as well as insects and large quantities of earthworms, which it roots out with its sensitive nose. It will also eat berries, nuts, and seeds. The badger is one of the few mustelids to live in family groups—it digs a network of underground passages and chambers called a sett.

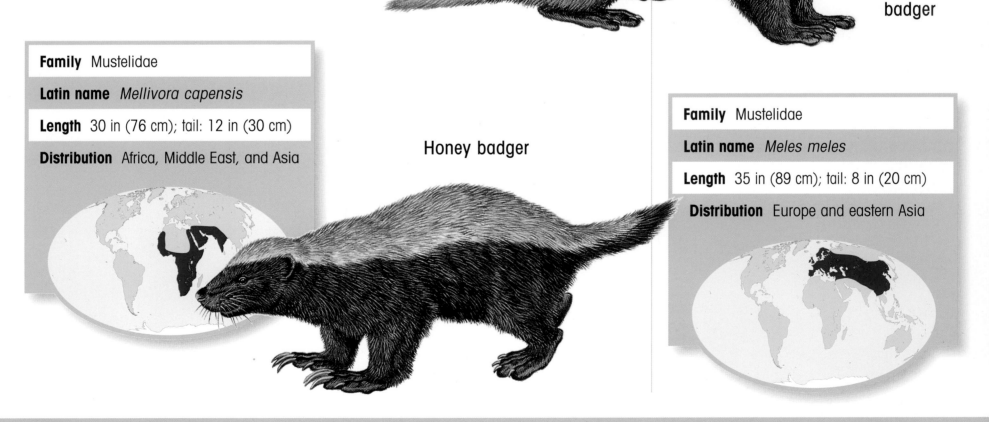

Eurasian badger

Honey badger

Family	Mustelidae
Latin name	*Mellivora capensis*
Length	30 in (76 cm); tail: 12 in (30 cm)
Distribution	Africa, Middle East, and Asia

Family	Mustelidae
Latin name	*Meles meles*
Length	35 in (89 cm); tail: 8 in (20 cm)
Distribution	Europe and eastern Asia

Striped skunk

This animal usually sleeps in a burrow or in a den under an old building or pile of logs during the day. At night, it comes out to hunt mice, birds, and insects and it will also scavenge in garbage cans for leftover food. The skunk can give off a foul-smelling liquid from glands near its tail but uses this against attackers, not prey.

Striped skunk

Family	Mustelidae
Latin name	*Mephitis mephitis*
Length	30 in (76 cm); tail: 10 in (25 cm)
Distribution	North America

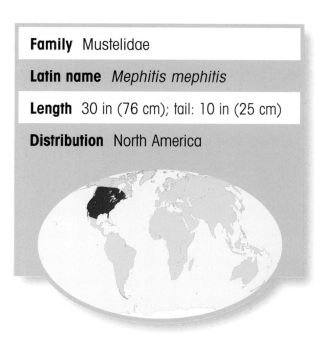

Sea otter

The sea otter feeds mostly on clams, mussels, and other shellfish and has found a way of dealing with their shells. When it gathers its prey on the seabed, it also picks up a rock. It lies on its back in the water with the rock on its chest and bangs its catch against the rock until the shell breaks. It then eats the soft flesh inside.

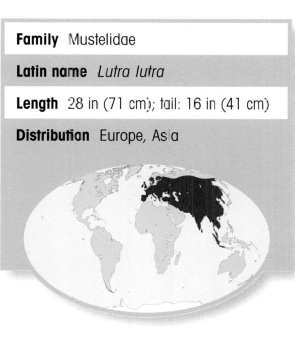

Sea otter

Family	Mustelidae
Latin name	*Enhydra lutris*
Length	4 ft (1.2 m); tail: 14½ in (37 cm)
Distribution	North Pacific coasts

Family	Mustelidae
Latin name	*Lutra lutra*
Length	28 in (71 cm); tail: 16 in (41 cm)
Distribution	Europe, Asia

European otter

The otter hunts on land and in water, preying on animals, such as rats, mice, and birds as well as fish and frogs. It generally seizes its prey in its mouth. In water, the otter's long whiskers help it hunt—they pick up any movements in the water made by prey.

European otter

Genets, linsangs, and mongooses

The civet family includes about 35 species of small carnivorous animals, such as genets, civets, and mongooses. Most are stealthy, catlike hunters, which catch a wide range of prey. They have sharp teeth and good senses of hearing, sight, and smell. The 39 species of mongooses are similar in appearance, with a long slender body and tail. They, too, are fast-moving hunters of small prey.

Small-spotted genet

As a slender, agile hunter, the genet moves fast and climbs well. It does prey on birds in the trees but generally stalks prey on the ground, crouching almost flat as it inches toward its victim, often a lizard or mouse.

Family	Viverridae
Latin name	*Genetta genetta*
Length	22 in (55 cm); tail: 20 in (51 cm)
Distribution	Western Europe, central and southern Africa

African linsang

African linsang

As an expert climber, this slender, forest-dwelling carnivore spends more time in the trees than on the ground. It sleeps during the day in a nest in the trees and wakes up at night to hunt prey, such as insects and young birds. It catches small vertebrate animals if it comes across them. The linsang is also known as the oyan.

Family	Viverridae
Latin name	*Poiana richardsoni*
Length	15 in (38 cm); tail: 14¼ in (36 cm)
Distribution	West and central Africa

Small-spotted genet

African civet

This civet is not fussy about its diet and eats a wide range of foods, including mice, reptiles, and birds as well as insects and birds' eggs. It can even eat things that might be poisonous to some animals, such as millipedes and rotting carrion. It picks up prey in its large teeth, not its paws, and kills small animals by shaking them until the neck breaks. This civet usually hunts on the ground, but will enter water and swims well.

Family	Viverridae
Latin name	*Civettictis civetta*
Length	35 in (89 cm); tail: 18½ in (47 cm)
Distribution	West and central Africa

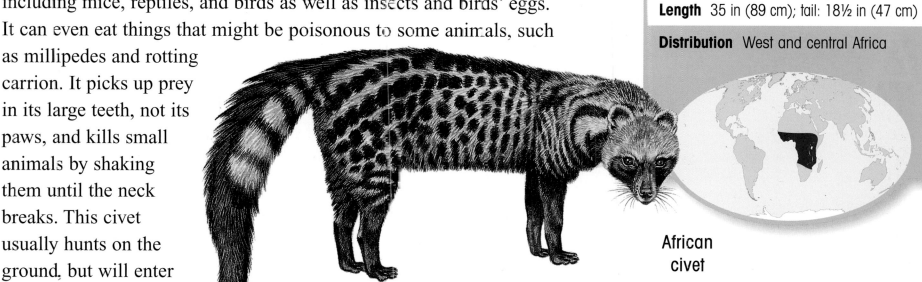

African civet

White-tailed mongoose

Family	Herpestidae
Latin name	*Ichneumia albicauda*
Length	28 in (71 cm); tail: 18½ in (47 cm)
Distribution	West and central Africa

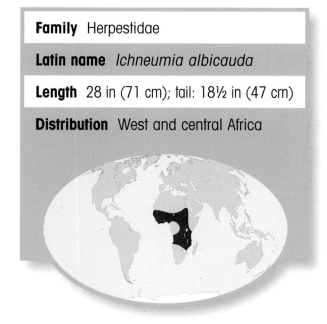

Large insects, such as locusts and beetles, are the main prey of this fast-moving mongoose, but it also hunts rats, lizards, snakes, and birds. It takes birds' eggs, too, and cracks them by throwing them against a rock or other hard object. One of its relatives, the Indian mongoose, is known to prey on large snakes, such as cobras, which it kills with a bite to the head.

White-tailed mongoose

Cusimanse

This little mongoose generally lives in groups. The mongooses forage on the ground for prey, such as insects and reptiles, by digging into the soil with their long snout and sharp claws. They often live around swampy land and so also feed on crabs, which they crack open against rocks.

Family	Herpestidae
Latin name	*Crossarchus obscurus*
Length	18 in (46 cm); tail: 10 in (25 cm)
Distribution	West Africa

Cusimanse

Scavengers

A scavenger is a meat-eater that usually feeds on the remains of dead animals. In this way, hyenas, vultures, and other scavengers clear up the remains of creatures that have died naturally from old age or illness, or have been left by predators. The scavengers are nature's garbage disposers and as such, perform a very important task in the natural world, where there is no room for waste.

Above Hyenas feed on the leftovers of other predators, but can also kill prey.

Scavengers in the sea

Crabs and other kinds of crustaceans have a varied diet and will eat anything they can find—animals or plants. They usually eat tiny scraps of food floating in the water, but also gobble up any dead fish and other creatures that drift down to the bottom of the sea. In this way, crabs help to keep the water clean.

Mini scavengers

There is also an army of much smaller scavengers, such as worms, beetles, and flies on land, and crabs and other crustaceans in the sea. Burying beetles, for example, certainly live up to their name. When the beetles find a dead animal, they sometimes dig away the soil under the body so it sinks into the ground. The beetles then lay their eggs on the carcass so when the eggs hatch, the young have a ready supply of food.

Some adult beetles also feed on dead animals. Carrion beetles feed on rotting flesh as well as maggots—fly larvae, which hatch from eggs laid on the carcass. Even smaller, are the huge numbers of bacteria, fungi, and single-celled animals that appear on the bodies of dead animals on the ground or in oceans and process them until there is nothing left and everything is recycled.

Sharing the feast

Vultures are some of the most efficient of the larger scavengers. They soar over the ground, searching for signs of food below. If a vulture spots a dead or dying animal, it drops to the ground to investigate. As soon as other vultures notice, they quickly join in and within minutes, a dead animal can be surrounded by squabbling birds, desperate for a share in the feast. It might look like a bloodthirsty scramble as the birds compete for a meal, but in fact, each type of vulture specializes in different parts of the body. The largest, such as the white-backed vultures, are strong enough to break open the body. They get the best bits of meat while smaller vultures have to wait their turn, and must be content with any scraps and bones that are left.

Hyenas and jackals take whatever food they can get and will kill prey as well as scavenge for food. Hyenas have amazingly powerful jaws and can crush bones and strip away skin and gristle very efficiently and so they make good use of almost every bit of a carcass. Jackals are smaller than hyenas. They usually arrive once the hyenas have opened up a carcass and dart in and out, snatching away whatever bits of meat they can. While some animals make scavenging a way of life, even such powerful hunters as lions and wolves will eat carrion if they get the chance.

Above White-backed and hooded vultures strip every remaining scrap of meat from a carcass.

Left The wily coyote will eat almost anything from fruit and insects to carrion and is always ready to scavenge for a meal.

Small cats

Cats are supreme hunters. There are about 38 species in the cat family, ranging from small creatures, such as wild cats and bobcats to the top predators— lions and tigers. Big or small, all the cats are very similar in appearance with a strong supple body and rounded head. They have curved claws for holding struggling prey and sharp teeth for delivering the killing bite.

Eurasian lynx

Ocelot

The ocelot lives in a variety of habitats from dense tropical forest to dry scrub. Active at night, it runs, jumps, and climbs well and, unlike many cats, is also a good swimmer. It hunts rabbits, mice, and lizards on the ground and chases monkeys and birds in the trees.

Family	Felidae
Latin name	*Felis pardalis*
Length	39 in (100 cm); tail: 18 in (46 cm)
Distribution	Southern U.S.A., Central and South America

Eurasian lynx

The lynx is a determined hunter—it preys on animals, such as deer, that are 3 or 4 times its size, but will also hunt smaller creatures, such as hares. It generally stalks its prey until it gets close to make a final high-speed dash and pounce. When food is plentiful, the lynx may hide some of its kills to come back to another time.

Family	Felidae
Latin name	*Felis lynx*
Length	4¼ ft (1.3 m); tail: 10 in (25 cm)
Distribution	Parts of Europe and Asia

Ocelot

Serval

The serval is a slender, lightly built cat with a small head and long neck and legs. It usually hunts at night, tracking prey, such as rats and mice, through long grass mostly by sound. Once it has found its victim, it pounces and traps its catch in its front paws.

Serval

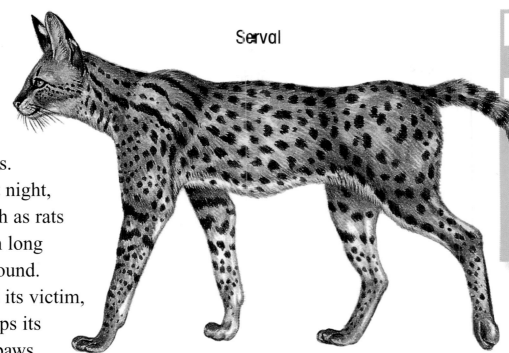

Family Felidae

Latin name *Felis serval*

Length 39 in (100 cm); tail: 18 in (46 cm)

Distribution Africa

Bobcat

The bobcat doesn't hesitate to tackle prey much larger than itself, such as deer, but also hunts smaller animals, such as rabbits, hares, and squirrels. It stalks its prey with great care, and then makes a speedy pounce for the kill. The bobcat gets its name from its little tail, which is much smaller than that of most of its relatives.

Family Felidae

Latin name *Lynx rufus*

Length 43 in (109 cm); tail: 7½ in (19 cm)

Distribution North America

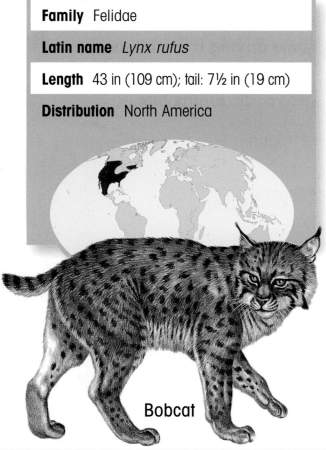

Bobcat

Caracal

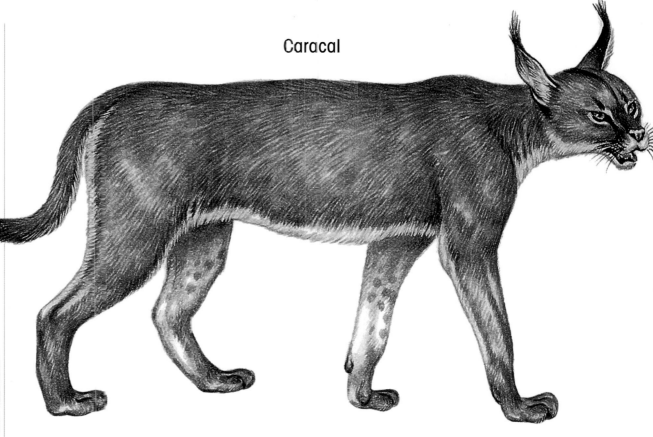

Caracal

This cat is also known as the desert lynx because of its tufted lynxlike ears. A speedy runner, it is probably the fastest cat of its size. It hunts at night, taking anything it can find from rats and mice to birds and monkeys. It is well-known for its ability to make leaps of up to 10 ft (3 m) into the air to snatch at birds with its sharp claws.

Family Felidae

Latin name *Caracal caracal*

Length 36 in (91 cm); tail: 12 in (30 cm)

Distribution Parts of Africa and Asia

Big cats

Hugely strong and powerful, the big cats really are the top predators in the animal kingdom. There are a few animals that they cannot overcome. But despite their fearsome reputation, these killers actually spend more time sleeping than hunting! They do not, however, need to catch prey every day.

Family	Felidae
Latin name	*Panthera leo*
Length	8¼ ft (2.5 m); tail: 3½ ft (1 m)
Distribution	Africa

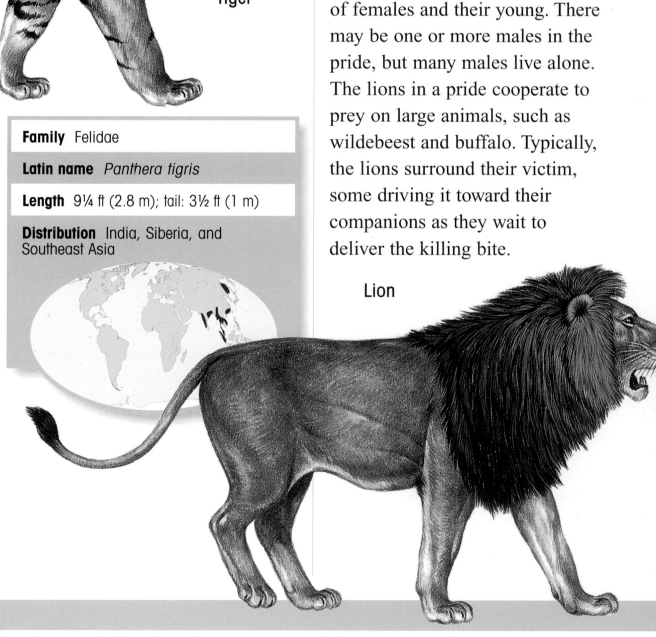

Tiger

Lion

Unlike other cats, the lion is a social animal and lives in groups called prides, based on a number of females and their young. There may be one or more males in the pride, but many males live alone. The lions in a pride cooperate to prey on large animals, such as wildebeest and buffalo. Typically, the lions surround their victim, some driving it toward their companions as they wait to deliver the killing bite.

Lion

Tiger

The tiger can run fast but only over short distances. It depends on stealth to get near enough to its prey before pouncing. The tiger's stripes help keep it hidden as it creeps up on prey, which it often tracks by smell and hearing rather than by sight. Once it is as close as possible, it rushes toward its victim and grasps its prey with a clawed paw before seizing the throat with its teeth. Deer and wild pigs are frequent prey, but the tiger also catches smaller creatures, such as birds and monkeys, and will enter water to catch fish.

Family	Felidae
Latin name	*Panthera tigris*
Length	9¼ ft (2.8 m); tail: 3½ ft (1 m)
Distribution	India, Siberia, and Southeast Asia

Jaguar

The largest South American cat, the jaguar, is a powerful creature. It cannot run fast for long distances so it stalks its prey, such as peccaries and capybaras, and gets as close as possible before going in for the kill. It also hunts birds, caimans, and fish and is a good swimmer.

Family	Felidae
Latin name	*Panthera onca*
Length	6¼ ft (1.9 m); tail: 30 in (76 cm)
Distribution	Central and northern South America

Jaguar

Leopard

Family	Felidae
Latin name	*Panthera pardus*
Length	6¼ ft (1.9 m); tail: 43 in (109 cm)
Distribution	Africa, south and southeast Asia

Antelopes, baboons, and monkeys are all favorite prey of the leopard, but it will also catch smaller prey, such as rats, mice, and even insects. This big cat is an agile climber and often drags its kill up into a tree where it can feed in peace.

Leopard

Clouded leopard

Perhaps the least known of all the larger cats, the clouded leopard is rarely seen. Its legs are particularly strong and it is thought to be an excellent climber, although it does most of its hunting on the ground. Birds, monkeys, goats, and deer are common prey. This cat also has particularly long canine teeth, much longer than those of other cats of its size.

Family	Felidae
Latin name	*Neofelis nebulosa*
Length	43 in (109 cm); tail: 36 in (91 cm)
Distribution	South and southeast Asia

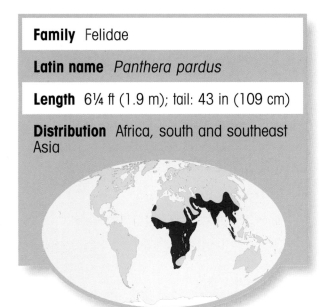

Clouded leopard

Capture by speed

To have a good chance of a successful kill, a predator must be stronger or faster than its prey, preferably both. On land, in the air, and in the ocean, many of the fastest-moving creatures are hunters, which rely on their speed to catch prey. Some speedy hunters succeed by being able to move very fast for short distances after having first crept as close as possible to their prey, while others, such as hunting dogs and wolves, might run at slightly slower speeds but can keep up the chase for mile after mile until their prey is exhausted.

Fast movers

The champion sprinter in the animal kingdom is the cheetah, which can run at speeds of up to 64 mph (103 km/h). But the cheetah cannot keep this pace up for long and so it depends on being able to stalk its prey and get as close as possible before making the final high-speed chase. Once the cheetah catches its prey, it seizes the victim by the throat to suffocate and kill the animal. Lions, too, can run fast for short distances.

Ocean hunters

With their sleek, streamlined bodies, dolphins are fast swimmers, which cut through the water like torpedoes. They have been timed swimming at speeds of up to 18 mph (30 km/h) as they pursue fish and squid. They can also continue at high speed for long distances. They must surface regularly to breath and sometimes make graceful leaps above the water's surface.

A lion's top speed may be less than that of many of its prey animals, such as gazelles, but it can reach that top speed more quickly, thanks to its muscular power. This means that over a short distance, the lion has a good chance of overtaking its prey.

Predatory birds can also move fast. The record breaker in level flight is the spine-tailed swift, which reaches 106 mph (170 km/h), while the peregrine falcon makes near-vertical dives at speeds of up to 200 mph (320 km/h) to strike its prey in midair. Some seabirds, such as gannets, make spectacular high-speed dives into the water to seize fish. It is much harder to move fast in water because water is 750 times more dense than air and so it requires far more effort. Typically, a fast swimming fish or mammal has a smooth, streamlined body that tapers at each end to minimize resistance. Champion ocean hunters include the marlin, which can swim at speeds of 50 mph (80 km/h), and the sailfish, which reaches speeds of 68 mph (109 km/h).

Above The amazing peregrine falcon flies at speeds of up to 69 mph (111 km/h) in level flight when chasing its prey through the air.

Above A cheetah nears the end of its high-speed chase as it closes in on a Thomson's gazelle.

Seals, sea lions, and walruses

Northern elephant seal

These mammals have become well adapted to life in water and have paddlelike flippers instead of legs. All are meat-eaters and prey on a variety of sea creatures. They spend much of their time in the sea and can dive to great depths but must still surface regularly to breathe air. Sea lions move more easily on land than seals, as they can tuck their back flippers under the body to help push themselves along.

Leopard seal

The most predatory of all the seals, the leopard seal hunts other seals and birds as well as fish and squid. It is the only seal that regularly kills warm-blooded prey. It has a large mouth and sharp teeth and can seize prey in the water as well as on land.

Leopard seal

Family	Phocidae
Latin name	*Hydrurga leptonyx*
Length	8¼–11 ft (2.5–3.3 m)
Distribution	Antarctic and subantarctic

Northern elephant seal

One of the largest of the seals, the male elephant seal weighs nearly 6,000 lb (2,700 kg). The female is only about half this size. Elephant seals have been known to dive as deep as nearly 5,000 ft (1,500 m) and stay underwater for 90 minutes. They hunt during their long, deep dives, catching mainly fish and squid.

Family	Phocidae
Latin name	*Mirounga angustirostris*
Length	6½–16½ ft (2–5 m)
Distribution	Pacific coast of North America

Walrus

The mighty walrus is a deep diver and finds most of its shellfish prey on the seabed. It uses its long sensitive whiskers to help it find food and manages to extract the flesh from the shellfish by means of a kind of suction action with its mouth and tongue. Walruses do also occasionally hunt seals and even whales. Their tusks are actually long canine teeth and can grow up to 3¼ ft (1 m) long. They are used in battles with rivals, not for finding food.

Family	Odobenidae
Latin name	*Odobenus rosmarus*
Length	7¼–12 ft (2.2–3.6 m)
Distribution	Arctic Ocean

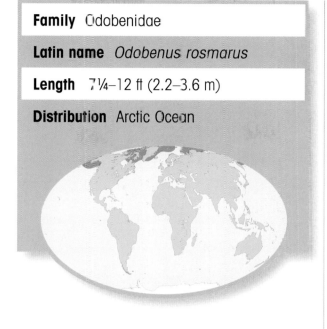

Walrus

Steller sea lion

The steller, the largest sea lion, feeds mainly on fish, but sometimes preys on young seals and sea otters. It needs to eat at least 6 percent of its body weight every day to survive but does not need to drink as its food provides all the liquid it needs. Its long whiskers help it find its way and help it search out prey in deep dark water.

Family	Otariidae
Latin name	*Eumetopias jubatus*
Length	9–10½ ft (2.7–3.2 m)
Distribution	North Pacific

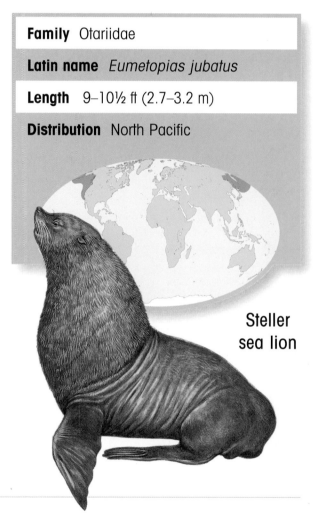

Steller
sea lion

South American fur seal

Fish and shrimp are the main food of the fur seal, which hunts mainly at night and dives to depths of 550 ft (170 m). Like most seals and sea lions, the fur seal swallows smaller prey whole, but chops larger kills into bite-sized pieces by shaking them in its jaws.

South American
fur seal

Family	Otariidae
Latin name	*Arctocephalus australis*
Length	5–6½ ft (1.5–2 m)
Distribution	South American coasts

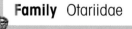

Whales

Whales, dolphins, and porpoises are the only mammals that spend their whole lives in water and never come to land. All are streamlined creatures with strong tails and flippers instead of limbs. There are two main types. Toothed whales include about 70 species of small whales, dolphins, and porpoises, all of which hunt sea creatures, such as fish and squid. The 12 species of baleen whales are very large animals, which filter huge quantities of small prey from the water.

Sei whale

Sei whale

The sei whale is a baleen whale and feeds mostly on small crustaceans, which it filters from the water through fringed plates that hang from its upper jaw. The whale also eats fish, which it catches by skimming the surface of the water with its open mouth.

Family	Balaenopteridae
Latin name	*Balaenoptera borealis*
Length	45–55 ft (13.7–16.7 m)
Distribution	Oceans worldwide

Northern bottlenose whale

This whale makes long deep dives for prey, such as squid, cuttlefish, and other bottom-living creatures as well as fish. It can stay down for up to 70 minutes and often dives to 3,300 ft (1,000 m) or deeper. Although the bottlenose is a toothed whale, its teeth are small and often so deeply embedded in the gums that they cannot be seen. It is thought to feed by a kind of suction method.

Family	Ziphiidae
Latin name	*Hyperoodon ampullatus*
Length	Up to 35 ft (10.6 m)
Distribution	North Atlantic

Northern bottlenose whale

Narwhal

Family	Monodontidae
Latin name	*Monodon monoceros*
Length	13–20 ft (4–6.1 m)
Distribution	Arctic Ocean

Sometimes known as the unicorn of the sea, the male narwhal has a long spiral tusk that can grow to 9 ft (2.7 m). The tusk is formed from a tooth that grows out through a hole in the upper lip. The male does not hunt with his tusk, but may use it to impress females or fight off rivals. The narwhal feeds on fish, squid, and crustaceans and probably sucks its prey into its mouth

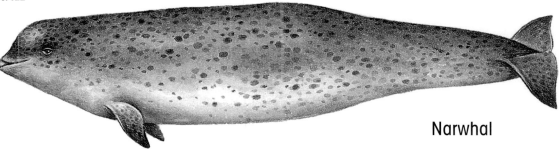

Narwhal

Pygmy sperm whale

This small toothed whale has an underslung lower jaw like a shark and 12–16 pairs of sharp curved teeth. It preys on squid, octopus fish, and shrimp and sometimes moves in small groups of up to five whales.

Family	Kogiidae
Latin name	*Kogia breviceps*
Length	9–10 ft (2.7–3 m)
Distribution	Oceans worldwide

Pygmy sperm whale

Gray whale

Family	Eschrichtiidae
Latin name	*Eschrichtius robustus*
Length	43–49 ft (13–15 m)
Distribution	North Pacific

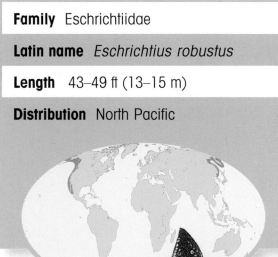

This is a baleen whale and, like its relatives, it feeds by filtering mouthfuls of water through rows of fringed plates that hang from its upper jaw. Any small creatures in the water are caught on the plates and the water is pushed out at the sides of the mouth. The whale then uses its tongue to push the food to the back of the mouth for swallowing.

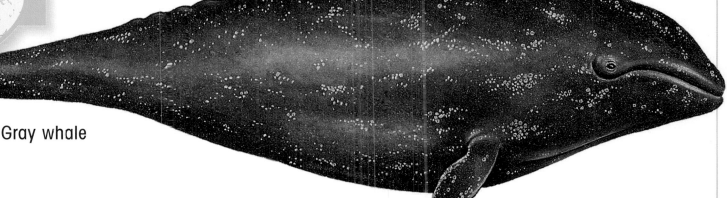

Gray whale

Dolphins and porpoises

Striped dolphin

These small toothed whales have a very special way of finding their prey. They use a kind of ultrasonic sonar, emitting high-frequency clicking sounds, which bounce off objects in their path. The echoes from these tell the whale about the size, distance, and speed of travel of the object. The animals also use echolocation to communicate with each other.

Killer whale

Also known as the orca and the wolf of the sea, this fierce whale is the largest of the dolphin family. It is well adapted for life as a predator with its large mouth and up to 50 teeth. These teeth point slightly backward and interlock, which helps the dolphin hold on to and tear apart its prey. It hunts a wide variety of creatures, including seals and sea lions, sharks, fish, penguins, and even other whales. Killer whales sometimes hunt in groups to herd their victims together for the kill. They also pursue seals right into shallow waters and have been seen tipping penguins and seals off ice floes.

Family	Delphinidae
Latin name	*Orcinus orca*
Length	Up to 32 ft (9.7 m)
Distribution	Worldwide

Striped dolphin

This dolphin usually lives in large groups of several hundred animals. It is a very agile, acrobatic creature and often makes leaps and spins above the water's surface. Fish and squid are its main prey.

Family	Delphinidae
Latin name	*Stenella coeruleoalba*
Length	7¼– 8 ft (2.2–2.4 m)
Distribution	Tropical and temperate waters worldwide

Killer whale

Long-finned pilot whale

Squid are the main prey of this dolphin and it may eat up to 30 lb (13.6 kg) of meat a day. These whales sometimes hunt in groups—they surround a school of squid and concentrate them into a small area so they are easier to gobble up. They also eat fish.

Family	Delphinidae
Latin name	*Globicephala melaena*
Length	Up to 20 ft (6.1 m)
Distribution	Cooler waters worldwide

Long-finned pilot whale

Amazon river dolphin

Family	Iniidae
Latin name	*Inia geoffrensis*
Length	6½–8½ ft (2–2.6 m)
Distribution	South America: Amazon basin

This river dolphin is also known as the boutu. It has a strong, thickset body and a long beak studded with up to 100 teeth. At the front of the mouth are sharp teeth, which are used for seizing prey, such as catfish and piranhas, while farther back are broad flat molars for crushing the food before swallowing. The dolphin's beak is also studded with short hairs, which may help it sense other prey, such as crustaceans.

Amazon river dolphin

Harbor porpoise

This porpoise preys on fish, such as herring and cod, which it tracks by echolocation and catches in its small spade-shaped teeth. It sometimes hunts in groups, particularly when preying on schooling fish. It can dive down to more than 655 ft (200 m).

Family	Phocoenidae
Latin name	*Phocoena phocoena*
Length	4½–6½ ft (1.4–2 m)
Distribution	North Pacific and Atlantic oceans, Black Sea

Harbor porpoise

Predatory primates

Although most monkeys and apes feed mainly on plant foods, such as leaves and fruit, primates do have some surprising eating habits. Many of the smaller members of the group, such as bush babies and the aye-aye, eat large numbers of insects as well as plants, and the tarsier feeds almost entirely on small prey. Chimpanzees and baboons actively hunt and kill large animals.

Above The tarsier eats insects, which it crunches up with its strong teeth.

Hunting for food

Baboons eat a wide range of food, including plants, insects, birds, and birds' eggs. They also hunt vertebrate animals up to the size of small antelopes. A baboon may hunt alone or in groups, stalking and chasing down its prey. Although gorillas and orangutans do gobble up insects along with leaves and sometimes eat other small creatures if they happen to come across them, they do not go hunting. Chimpanzees, on the other hand, are skilled killers, which prey on other mammals, such as monkeys and bush pigs. They generally hunt in a pack—females and young chimpanzees may help to drive prey toward the larger male chimps who make the kill. The catch is then shared out between the group, though the males get the biggest share of the meat.

"Fishing" for ants and termites

Insects are an important part of a chimpanzee's diet, and this primate has discovered how to use sticks to "fish" for a favorite snack of ants and termites. The chimpanzee finds a suitable twig, strips off the leaves, and uses it to probe into the insects' nest. The insects immediately swarm onto the intruding object to investigate it. The chimp then quickly pulls the stick out of the nest and licks off the tasty insects.

49

Birds

Birds live in every type of habitat, from deserts and tropical rain forests to polar regions. There are more than 9,000 species, possibly as many as 10,000, ranging in size from tiny hummingbirds to ostriches that stand taller than an adult human. Most birds can fly and a typical bird has a light but strong body, two legs, and a pair of wings. All birds are covered with feathers, which keep them warm and streamline their bodies for flight.

Below Prey can be hard to come by in a winter storm. This white-tailed eagle is trying to drive a golden eagle away from its kill in order to steal it.

What birds eat

Some birds feed only on plant foods, but many catch and eat other creatures. Some are expert insect predators—swifts, for example, chase their prey through the air with great agility. Others, such as hawks, eagles, and owls, catch much larger prey, which they seize in their strong claws. Many birds feed on fish, which they catch by making spectacular dives into the water or pursuing their prey beneath the surface. All birds have a beak with which they can pick up food or tear it apart and beaks vary in shape according to diet. Birds of prey, for example, have large hooked beaks for tearing into flesh, while the beaks of insect eaters are fine and slender.

Owls

There are around 200 species of owls, all perfectly adapted for life as nighttime hunters. Typically, an owl sits on a branch watching and listening for the slightest movement of prey. When it hears something, it pinpoints the direction of the prey with its amazingly sharp hearing before flying down to pounce on its victim.

Tawny owl

Snowy owl

Tawny owl

Like all owls, the tawny owl has feathers with soft, fluffy edges, not hard like those of most birds. This cuts down the noise of flight so the owl can fly almost silently in darkness. Strictly nocturnal, the tawny owl sleeps in a tree during the day and hunts rats and mice, birds, and some insects at night.

Snowy owl

The snowy owl hunts during the day as well as at night and preys on mammals, such as lemmings and hares, as well as other birds. Its hearing is so good it can even hear a lemming tunneling under snow and it may eat up to five lemmings a day. Snowy owls have also been seen lying near water and snatching fish with their talons.

Family Strigidae

Latin name *Nyctea scandiaca*

Length 20½–28 in (52–71 cm)

Distribution Arctic tundra

Family Strigidae

Latin name *Strix aluco*

Length 14½–15½ in (37–39 cm)

Distribution Europe, Asia, northwest Africa

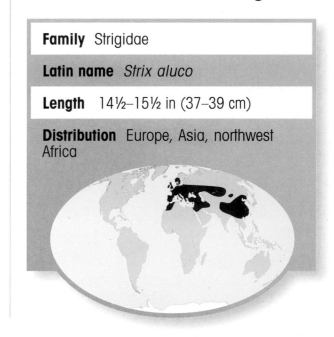

Family	Strigidae
Latin name	*Bubo virginianus*
Length	18–24¾ in (46–63 cm)
Distribution	North, Central, and South America

Great horned owl

The great horned owl is a large, powerful bird and a fierce predator. It often kills other owls and is one of the few creatures that preys on skunks. It kills with its sharp talons and tears prey apart with its hooked beak.

Great horned owl

Burrowing owl

This owl lives in burrows on the ground, often those left by prairie dogs and other mammals. It adapts the burrow to its needs by digging with its feet to enlarge it and make a nesting chamber. It usually hunts in the evening but is often seen at the entrance of its burrow in the daytime. Rodents, birds, frogs, and insects are its main prey.

Family	Strigidae
Latin name	*Athene cunicularia*
Length	7½–9¾ in (19–25 cm)
Distribution	North, Central, and South America

Burrowing owl

Oriental bay owl

This owl is a close relative of the barn owl and like the barn owl has a heart-shaped facial disk and long slender legs. The bay owl is strictly nocturnal and is thought to feed mainly on insects, which it hunts in and around trees.

Family	Tytonidae
Latin name	*Phodilus badius*
Length	9–13 in (23–33 cm)
Distribution	India and Southeast Asia

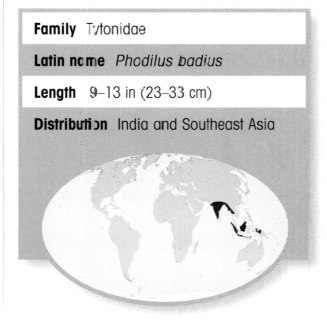

Oriental bay owl

Birds of prey 1

These are the most predatory of all birds and the most expert hunters. They range from tiny falcons to huge eagles, but all have very keen vision, strong feet with sharp claws, and a hooked beak for tearing flesh. Most kill with their feet, not with their beak.

Harpy eagle

Golden eagle

This huge powerful bird has several different ways of hunting its prey. It may soar for hours, ready to spot a rabbit or other animal below with its exceptionally keen eyes. It may also wait on a perch, dropping down to seize a victim in its talons. Alternatively, the eagle sometimes flies low over the ground searching for animals, such as prairie dogs. Hares and rabbits are frequent prey, but it can also manage to catch much larger animals, such as goats and deer.

Family	Accipitridae
Latin name	*Aquila chrysaetos*
Length	30–35 in (76–89 cm)
Distribution	North America, Europe, Asia, north Africa

Golden eagle

Harpy eagle

The harpy is the world's largest eagle. It has shorter, broader wings than most eagles and does not soar high above the ground searching for prey like most eagles. Instead, it hunts in the rain forest canopy and chases its prey though the trees at speeds of up to 50 mph (80 km/h). Monkeys are a favorite prey and the harpy also hunts sloths, porcupines, snakes, and iguanas.

Family	Accipitridae
Latin name	*Harpia harpyja*
Length	35–39 in (89–100 cm)
Distribution	Central and South America

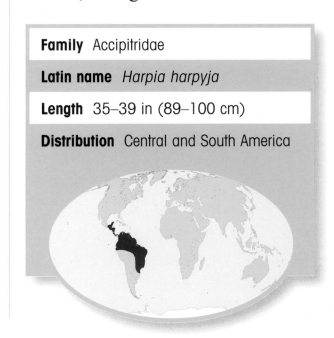

Bald eagle

The majestic bald eagle often lives near water and is skilled at snatching fish with its clawed talons. It will also feed on dead or dying fish, such as exhausted migrating salmon. It preys on mammals, such as muskrats and hares, as well as waterbirds and gulls. It will also steal prey from other eagles and feed on carrion and garbage.

Bald eagle

Family	Accipitridae
Latin name	Haliaeetus leucocephalus
Length	28–38 in (71–96.5 cm)
Distribution	North America

Martial eagle

The martial is the largest eagle in Africa and is an incredibly powerful bird. It preys on other birds, such as bustards and guinea fowl, and also hunts mammals, such as small antelopes, moneys, and goats, and it attacks snakes and lizards. It spends much of its time in the air and does most of its hunting by soaring high above the ground, then diving down at high speed for the kill. The female is larger than the male.

Martial eagle

Family	Accipitridae
Latin name	Polemaetus bellicosus
Length	31–34 in (79–86 cm)
Distribution	Africa

Bateleur

This beautiful bird of prey is part of the group known as snake eagles, but it feeds mostly on carrion. It also makes fierce attacks on other carrion-eating birds and robs them of their spoils. The bateleur does hunt its own prey, too, including ground birds, lizards, and hares. It is a spectacular bird in flight—it soars for hours and may travel 200 miles (320 km) every day.

Bateleur

Family	Accipitridae
Latin name	Terathopius ecaudatus
Length	24 in (61 cm)
Distribution	Africa

Birds of prey 2

These smaller birds of prey are as skilled at hunting as their larger relatives. Like eagles, these hawks and falcons have keen senses and deadly weapons in the form of talons and hooked beaks. Some, such as the snail kite, have very special methods of tackling their prey.

Long-legged buzzard

Northern goshawk

This large aggressive hawk is an efficient killer. It flies through the forest, weaving in and out of the trees, and sometimes soars over the treetops. It kills with a vicelike grip of its powerful talons, driving them into its prey, and then eats its catch on the ground. It plucks its bird kills before eating. The goshawk also sometimes stalks prey on the ground and can tackle birds as large as pheasants and grouse and mammals the size of rabbits and hares. Female goshawks are up to 50 percent larger than males.

Family Accipitridae

Latin name *Accipiter gentilis*

Length 19–28 in (48–71 cm)

Distribution North America, Europe, northern Asia

Northern goshawk

Long-legged buzzard

Like other buzzards, this bird of prey hovers in the sky as it watches prey on the ground below, then plummets down to attack. It generally flies over mountainous areas and preys on lizards and small mammals.

Family Accipitridae

Latin name *Buteo rufinus*

Length 20–26 in (51–66 cm)

Distribution Eastern Europe, central Asia, north Africa

Gyrfalcon

Gyrfalcon

This powerful hunter is the biggest of the falcons—it can catch birds the size of grouse and ducks. It has several ways of hunting. It may perch on a high spot watching for prey, fly low over the ground and make a rapid dive toward its kill, or chase prey in the air. It tends to drive its victim to the ground before killing rather than attack in the air. Ptarmigan, grouse, and ducks are common prey and the gyrfalcon also catches hares, squirrels, and lemmings.

Family	Falconidae
Latin name	*Falco rusticolus*
Length	20–23 in (51–58 cm)
Distribution	North America, northern Europe and Asia

Eurasian hobby

The fast-flying hobby catches almost all of its prey on the wing and is one of the most agile of aerial hunters. Other speedy fliers, such as swifts and swallows, are frequent prey and it also catches insects and bats. It seizes prey in its talons and then transfers the prey to its beak while in the air.

Family	Falconidae
Latin name	*Falco subbuteo*
Length	12–14 in (30–35.5 cm)
Distribution	Europe, Africa, Asia, parts of North America

Eurasian hobby

Snail kite

This kite feeds almost entirely on freshwater snails and has a long thin upper beak for dealing with its prey. It flies slowly over the water until it spots a snail, then hovers while it grasps the prey in its talons—it never plunges into the water or takes the snails with its beak. It then flies back to a perch and stands on one foot while holding the snail in the other. It inserts its narrow beak into the shell, cuts the muscle that holds the snail in place, pulls out the flesh, and shakes the shell off. The shell is then dropped to the ground.

Snail kite

Family	Accipitridae
Latin name	*Rostrhamus sociabilis*
Length	14–15½ in (35.5–39 cm)
Distribution	Southeast U.S.A., Central and South America

Birds of prey—the hunting experts

Birds of prey, such as eagles, hawks, and falcons, are the most exciting of all birds. Buzzards and eagles soar for miles over open country, searching for signs of prey below and then drop down to kill their victims with their sharp clawed feet. Others, such as goshawks, hunt in forests. They fly from perch to perch, ready to glide swiftly to the ground to catch prey. Fish eagles hunt over water and swoop down to the surface to seize fish in their talons.

Above This northern hawk owl flies up from snowy ground with a rat firmly grasped in its strong talons.

Beaks and feet

The sharp clawed feet of birds of prey are their main weapons and most kill with their feet, not their beaks. The upper part of the beak is hooked and pointed for tearing prey apart as the bird eats. Owls also have sharp beaks and talons. They hunt mostly at night and although they do have excellent vision, they also depend on their good hearing to help them find prey in complete darkness. An owl can pinpoint the source of the tiniest sound, helping it to make a precise attack and swoop and grab its victim in its talons. An owl's soft-edged feathers are another adaptation for hunting at night. These make much less noise in flight than the normal hard-edged feathers of other birds of prey and so enable the owl to approach its victim almost silently.

A hovering kestrel

Smaller birds of prey, such as kestrels, hover above the ground as they search for prey. The kestrel, which is a kind of falcon, can stay up in the air and remain in one spot by beating its wings very fast as it scans the ground below. When it sees prey, the kestrel gradually comes down to the ground, before making a final pounce and seizing the creature in its clawed feet. The kestrel also sometimes catches other birds in midair or hunts from a perch high on a tree.

Above This African fish eagle swoops
down to snatch prey in its talons.
It also steals prey from other birds.

Vultures

Vultures are flesh-eating birds, but they do not always kill their prey. They are scavengers and generally feed on creatures that are already dead. They soar overland on their long, broad wings searching for food. Some use their excellent sense of smell as well as their keen eyesight to find carrion.

Lammergeier

Lappet-faced vulture

This bird is the largest and most powerful African vulture. It has the largest beak of any bird of prey and is the dominant bird among a group of vultures at a carcass. Indeed, the others often wait for the lappet-faced vulture to arrive and open up the carcass with its strong beak. It also preys on birds and may also kill mammals, such as young gazelles.

Lappet-faced vulture

Family	Accipitridae
Latin name	*Torgos tracheliotus*
Length	39–41 in (100–104 cm)
Distribution	Parts of Africa and Middle East

Lammergeier

Also known as the bearded vulture, the lammergeier lives in remote mountainous regions. It spends most of its day on the wing and soars for miles with seemingly effortless grace. It feeds on carrion of all sorts but must give way to larger vultures at carcasses. As the last to the food, the lammergeier is often left with the bones and has developed the knack of dropping them onto rocks to split them open and reveal the marrow inside.

Family	Accipitridae
Latin name	*Gypaetus barbatus*
Length	3¼–4 ft (1–1.2 m)
Distribution	Parts of southern Europe, Asia, and Africa

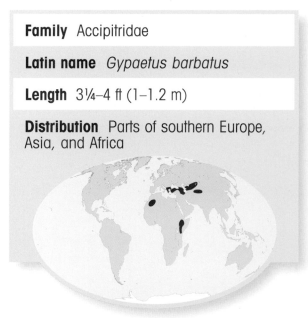

King vulture

This bird belongs to the New World vulture family, which is a quite separate group from the Old World vultures, such as the Egyptian and lappet-faced. But both groups of birds feed mostly on carrion and have features, such as bare heads, which allow them to plunge into messy carcasses without soiling their feathers. The king's head is marked with very colorful patterns and it has a strong hooked beak that is ideally shaped for tearing open carcasses. As its name suggests, this bird gets first choice at a kill and other birds give way when it arrives. It is thought to have a particularly good sense of smell that helps it find carrion in the dense rain forests where it lives. It also picks up stranded fish on riverbanks.

Family	Cathartidae
Latin name	*Sarcoramphus papa*
Length	27–32 in (68.5–81 cm)
Distribution	Central and South America

King vulture

Egyptian vulture

The Egyptian is the smallest vulture and must give way to larger relatives at carcasses so it is often left with scraps. It also preys on insects and other small creatures and eats ostrich eggs. As one of the few creatures to use a tool when feeding, this vulture has learned the trick of dropping rocks onto an egg to break open the hard shell.

Family	Accipitridae
Latin name	*Neophron percnopterus*
Length	23–28 in (58–71 cm)
Distribution	Europe, Africa, Asia

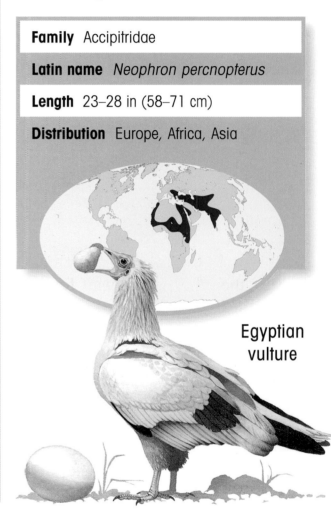

Egyptian vulture

Family	Cathartidae
Latin name	*Cathartes aura*
Length	25–32 in (63.5–81 cm)
Distribution	North, Central, and South America

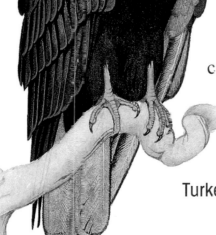

Turkey vulture

Turkey vulture

Also known as the turkey buzzard, this bird occurs over a wide area and adapts to habitats from deserts to rain forests. It feeds mostly on carrion, including road kills. Like other vultures, it has a good sense of smell, which helps it find food. It does also take live prey, particularly creatures that are trapped, sick, or injured.

Penguins and auks

Penguins live in the southern half of the world and auks in the north. The birds are not related but look similar because they live in much the same way—swimming, diving, and hunting fish. All penguins are flightless however, while auks can fly, except for a brief period when molting. There are about 17 species of penguins and 23 species of auks.

Family	Spheniscidae
Latin name	*Aptenodytes patagonicus*
Length	Up to 30 in (76 cm) tall
Distribution	Coasts of subantarctic islands

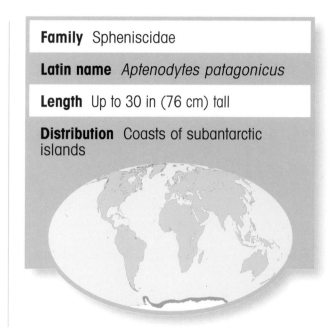

Emperor penguin

The emperor is the largest penguin and is perfectly adapted for life in the sea. Its wings have become paddles for swimming and its short, densely packed feathers keep it warm and dry in Antarctic waters. Its webbed feet are placed so far back on the body that it has to walk upright on land. It feeds mostly on fish, squid, and crustaceans, which it catches in deep dives. It is known to dive to more than 700 ft (213 m) and stay down for up to 18 minutes.

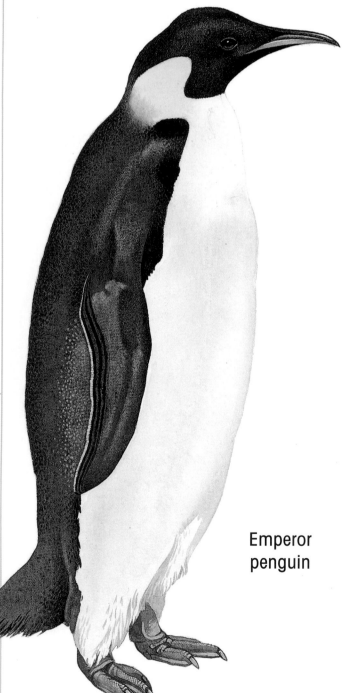

Emperor penguin

Family	Spheniscidae
Latin name	*Aptenodytes forsteri*
Length	Up to 40 in (101 cm) tall
Distribution	Antarctica

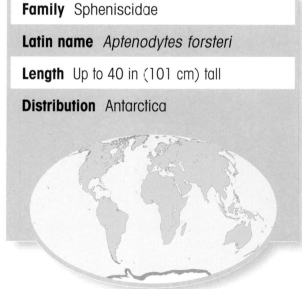

King penguin

The king penguin dives deep for prey, such as squid. It often plunges to 150 ft (45 m) or more and can stay underwater for 15 minutes before coming up for air. This penguin's main enemies are leopard seals and killer whales who lie in wait near the shore for unsuspecting birds to dive into the water.

King penguins

African penguin

Also known as the jackass penguin because of its braylike call, this bird used to be very common but its numbers are now greatly reduced. Small fish, such as anchovies and pilchards, are its main prey and these have been over fished to such an extent that the penguins are struggling to find food.

Family	Spheniscidae
Latin name	*Spheniscus demersus*
Length	Up to 26½ in (67 cm)
Distribution	Coasts of South Africa

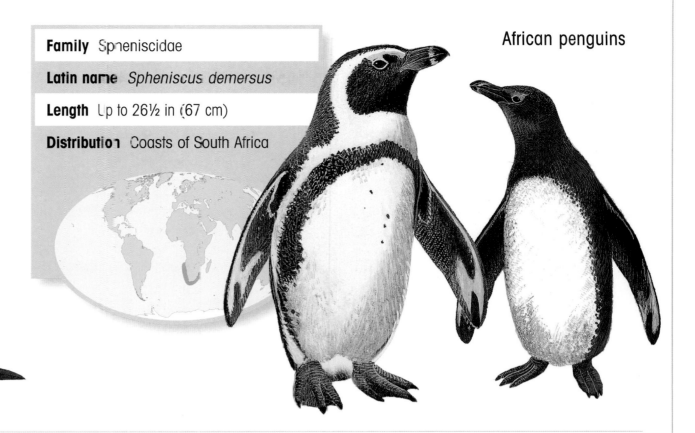

African penguins

Guillemot

Guillemot

The guillemot, also known as the common murre, is a member of the auk family. Like all auks, it is a truly marine bird and only comes to land to breed. It swims well and dives from the surface to pursue prey underwater, propelling itself with its short narrow wings. Fish, particularly sand eels, squid, and small crustaceans are its main prey and it usually eats underwater, although it may bring larger items to the surface to eat.

Family	Alcidae
Latin name	*Uria aalge*
Length	15½–16½ in (39–42 cm)
Distribution	North Atlantic and North Pacific

Atlantic puffin

This small auk has a large head and a spectacular striped beak, which it uses to catch food as well as for displaying to mates in the breeding season. Like other auks, the puffin catches fish in water and it may carry several in its beak while it snatches up more. Schooling fish, such as sand eels, whiting, and herring are common prey and the Atlantic puffin often hunts in shallow coastal waters.

Family	Alcidae
Latin name	*Fratercula arctica*
Length	11–12 in (28–30 cm)
Distribution	North Atlantic

Atlantic puffin

Albatrosses and relatives

S eabirds, such as albatrosses and petrels, spend much of their lives flying over the sea and they catch all their food in the water. Most are strong fliers as well as expert swimmers and divers and they have a dense coat of feathers to protect them from the cold and wet.

Wandering albatross

Wandering albatross

This huge seabird has one of the widest wingspans of any bird—tip to tip its wings measure up to 11 ft (3.3 m). It spends much of its life soaring over the ocean, and sometimes flies up to 310 miles (500 km) in a day. To hunt, it lands on the sea and seizes fish and squid from the surface waters in its beak. It also follows ships and feeds on waste thrown overboard.

Family	Diomedeidae
Latin name	*Diomedea exulans*
Length	Up to 3½ ft (1 m)
Distribution	Southern oceans

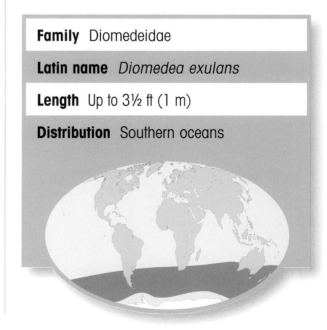

Light-mantled albatross

This small albatross has long narrow wings and is very graceful and agile in flight. It feeds mostly on squid and small crustaceans but also eats fish and carrion. It hunts by diving down from the water's surface and seizing prey in its strong beak.

Family	Diomedeidae
Latin name	*Phoebetria palpebrata*
Length	Up to 31½ in (80 cm)
Distribution	Southern oceans

Light-mantled albatross

European storm petrel

The storm petrel is one of the smallest European seabirds. It feeds mainly on fish and squid, which it catches as it swoops low over the water. It bounces over the sea with its feet touching the water as it feeds at the surface. Like many seabirds, it also follows ships and eats any food scraps thrown overboard.

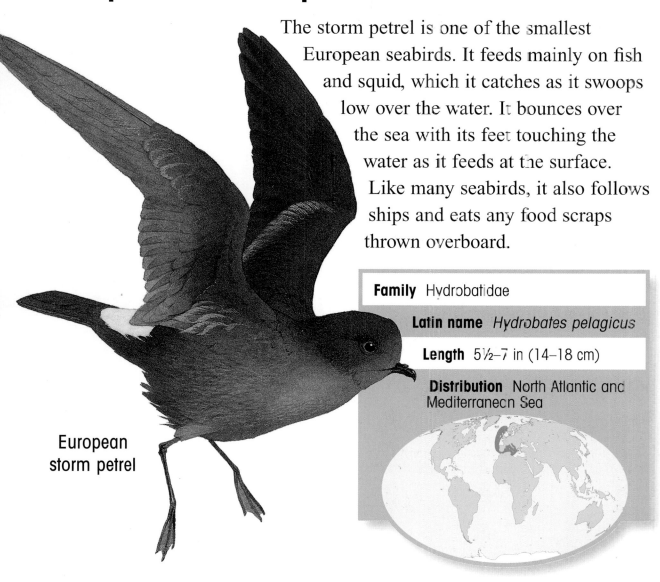

European storm petrel

Family Hydrobatidae

Latin name *Hydrobates pelagicus*

Length 5½–7 in (14–18 cm)

Distribution North Atlantic and Mediterranean Sea

Snowy sheathbill

The sheathbill does not have webbed feet and cannot swim and dive like true seabirds. Instead, this aggressive bird scavenges for much of its food, seizing dead fish and other debris from the shore and taking afterbirths and weak young from seal and penguin colonies. Sheathbills have even been seen stealing food from penguins as they feed their chicks.

Snowy sheathbill

Manx shearwater

This shearwater feeds mostly on small fish as well as squid and crustaceans. It hunts by seizing prey from surface waters or diving down and chasing fish underwater. It can also make short dives from the air.

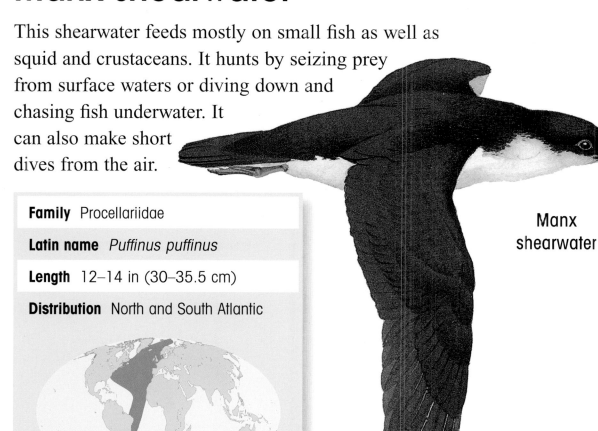

Manx shearwater

Family Procellariidae

Latin name *Puffinus puffinus*

Length 12–14 in (30–35.5 cm)

Distribution North and South Atlantic

Family Chionididae

Latin name *Chionis alba*

Length 13½–16 in (34–41 cm)

Distribution Southern South America and Antarctic peninsula

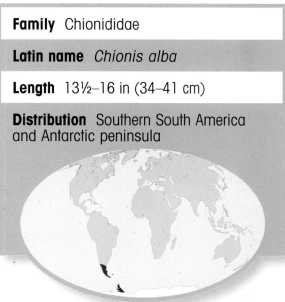

Gannets, gulls, and pelicans

A ll these seabirds are expert marine predators. Some, such as terns, gannets, and pelicans, dive from the sky to catch fish. Cormorants pursue their prey under the water, while skuas have a very different way of hunting—usually stealing from other birds.

Northern gannet

Great cormorant

The largest of the cormorant family, the great cormorant feeds mostly on fish but also eats frogs and crustaceans. It catches its prey by diving down from the water's surface, sometimes as deep as 115 ft (35 m). It can swim fast underwater in pursuit of its prey, using its webbed feet to push itself along and its long tail as a rudder. Most prey is brought back to the surface and shaken before being swallowed.

Great cormorant

Family	Phalacrocoracidae
Latin name	*Phalacrocorax carbo*
Length	31–39¼ in (79–100 cm)
Distribution	Eastern North America, Europe, Asia, southern Africa

Northern gannet

Gannets live in huge noisy colonies on cliffs and islands. This strong bird has a streamlined body and a thick neck. An expert in the air, it flies over water searching for signs of fish or squid. Once it spots its prey, the gannet dives 100 ft (30 m) or more down to the sea to grasp the catch in its daggerlike beak and bring the prey to the surface. The bird's strong beak and specially adapted skull takes much of the impact as it hits the surface. Also, its nostril openings are covered by bony flaps so water is not forced into them when the bird dives.

Family	Sulidae
Latin name	*Morus bassanus*
Length	32–35 in (81–89 cm)
Distribution	North Atlantic and Mediterranean Sea

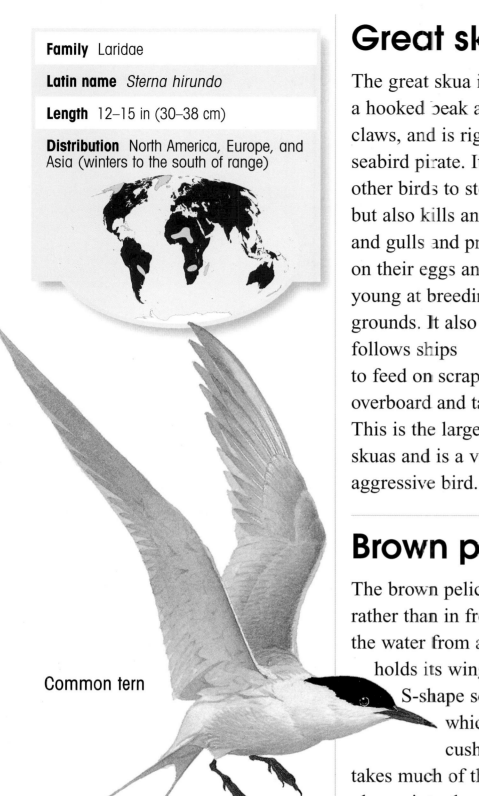

Family Laridae

Latin name *Sterna hirundo*

Length 12–15 in (30–38 cm)

Distribution North America, Europe, and Asia (winters to the south of range)

Common tern

Common tern

Fish, squid, and crustaceans are the main foods of the tern, which is a member of the gull family. This beautiful fast-flying bird hovers over the sea until it spots something, then dives into the water to seize the prey in its sharp beak. It flies back up into the air and swallows the prey seconds later. It also catches insects in the air and steals food from other terns.

Great skua

The great skua is a strong bird with a hooked beak and sharp, curved claws, and is rightly known as a seabird pirate. It not only attacks other birds to steal their prey, but also kills and eats ducks and gulls and preys on their eggs and young at breeding grounds. It also follows ships to feed on scraps thrown overboard and takes carrion. This is the largest of the skuas and is a very aggressive bird.

Family Stercorariidae

Latin name *Catharacta skua*

Length 20–23 in (51–58 cm)

Distribution Parts of South America, Europe, Africa, and Australia

Great skua

Brown pelican

The brown pelican is the smallest of its family and lives on sea coasts rather than in freshwater like other pelicans. It catches fish by diving into the water from as high as 50 ft (15 m). As it dives, it holds its wings back and its neck curved into an S-shape so that the front of the body, which is provided with cushioning airs sacs, takes much of the impact of the plunge into the water. The bird generally returns to the surface to eat its catch.

Family Pelecanidae

Latin name *Pelecanus occidentalis*

Length 3¼–5 ft (1–1.5 m)

Distribution North, Central, and South America and Caribbean

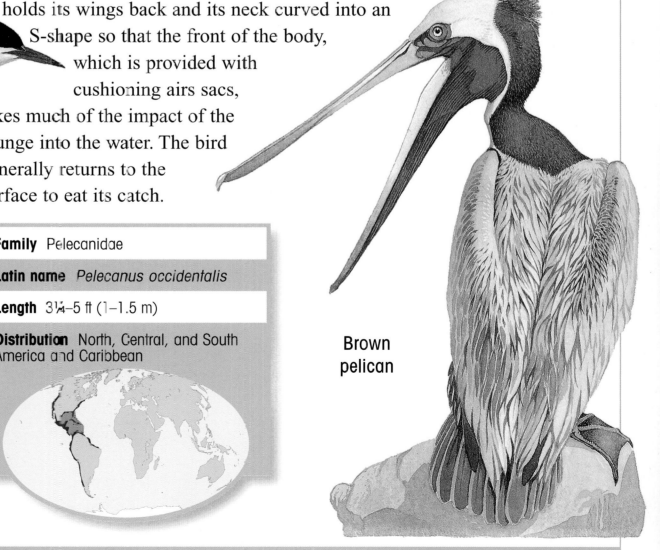

Brown pelican

Right The brown pelican dives into the sea, opens its mouth, and catches fish in the pouch under its beak.

Fishing for food

Some mammals, such as seals and whales, eat fish and even a few reptiles, but a huge range of birds, including seabirds and freshwater species, live almost entirely on fish. Many are expert swimmers and some are also superb divers. Their feathers make a dense, waterproof cover and many have webbed feet that they can use as paddles in the water.

How birds catch fish

Terns and gannets plunge out of the sky into the water to catch fish, while others, including puffins, dive down from the surface. Cormorants chase fish under the water until they are close enough to catch the prey in their hooked beaks. Penguins are the best swimmers of all and can dive deep and stay underwater for up to 18 minutes. Not all seabirds swim and dive to catch their food, however. Some storm petrels swoop down from the air and skim close to the water's surface to scoop up prey in their beaks. Seabirds have different shaped beaks according to how they catch their food. Terns and gannets have straight sharp beaks for cutting through the water and seizing prey. Underwater hunters, such as penguins, also have straight beaks. The puffin's broad beak is perfect for carrying fish back to land.

Above When a kingfisher dives into the water for fish, it holds its wings tightly folded back against its body.

Freshwater birds have their own ways of fishing. The bittern moves slowly through marshland or shallow water with its beak held ready to spear fish or crabs. The black heron stands in shallow water with its head down and its wings spread in a circle like a canopy over its head. This provides a patch of shade, which may make it easier for the bird to see prey in the water and may even attract fish to the area. The kingfisher sits on a perch above a stream and watches for fish. When it sees something, it plunges into the water, seizes its prey, and is back to the surface in seconds.

A fish-eating bat

There is even a bat that preys on fish. The greater bulldog bat, which lives in Central and South America, hunts over water at night. It uses echolocation to find ripples made by fish on the water's surface. It then swoops down to within an inch of the water, dipping briefly to snatch prey in its clawed back feet and scoop the fish into its mouth.

Herons and other waterbirds

A huge range of birds lives in and around lakes, rivers, and ponds. There is plenty of food for them in the water and there is also shelter on the banks where they can hide and nest. Herons and egrets belong to a family of about 60 species, all with long beaks, which they use for seizing prey. The 19 species of storks also have long beaks and hunt in water. Some of the 150 or so kinds of ducks feed on plants but others hunt for their food.

Gray heron

Gray heron

This large, long-legged bird has a big, sharp-tipped beak. It feeds on a wide range of prey, including fish, eels, young birds, small mammals, and snakes, as well as smaller creatures, such as insects and shellfish. It stands in shallow water or at the water's edge, then when it sees a movement, leans forward and grabs the prey with a swift lethal thrust of its strong beak.

Family	Ardeidae
Latin name	*Ardea cinerea*
Length	35–39 in (89–100 cm)
Distribution	Europe, Asia, Africa

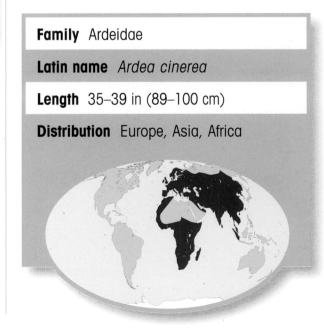

Great egret

The elegant great egret is a member of the heron family and, like herons, it has a long, daggerlike beak. Fish are its main prey, but it also catches frogs, small mammals, and crustaceans. It stands and waits in shallow water for passing prey or slowly stalks anything it sees, then seizes the creature with a swift movement of its beak. The egret will sometimes enter the water and swim in pursuit of prey but this is unusual.

Family	Ardeidae
Latin name	*Ardea alba*
Length	37–41 in (94–104 cm)
Distribution	North, Central, and South America, Africa, Asia, and Australia

Great egret

Sunbittern

The sunbittern lives around woodland streams and creeks where its mottled plumage helps to keep it hidden in the dappled light. It hunts by walking slowly and carefully through the shallows or along the water's edge, searching for fish, frogs, and crustaceans. Prey is seized with a swift thrust of its sharp spearlike beak.

Sunbittern

Family	Eurypygidae
Latin name	*Eurypyga helias*
Length	17–19 in (43–48 cm)
Distribution	Central and northern South America

White stork

The white stork is not a fussy eater and will eat anything that comes its way, including insects, frogs and tadpoles, fish, mice, snakes, lizards, and insects. It usually hunts by walking along with its beak pointing down to the ground. If it spots something, it jerks its head back, then jabs its beak down to catch the prey.

White stork

Family	Ciconiidae
Latin name	*Ciconia ciconia*
Length	39 in (100 cm)
Distribution	Parts of Europe, Africa, and Asia

Red-breasted merganser

The merganser, a fish-eating, diving duck, has a long thin beak, lined with sharp toothlike projections, which is ideal for catching fish in water. The duck makes brief dives from the surface to catch its prey. Mergansers also sometimes hunt in groups, driving schools of fish into tight groups in shallow water to make them easier to catch.

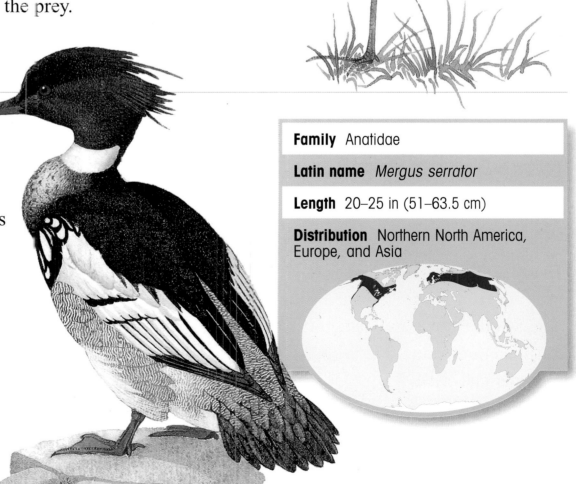

Red-breasted merganser

Family	Anatidae
Latin name	*Mergus serrator*
Length	20–25 in (51–63.5 cm)
Distribution	Northern North America, Europe, and Asia

Crows and other songbirds

Rook

The songbirds range from tiny wrens to sturdy ravens and have many different lifestyles. Some eat mainly seeds, fruit, nuts, and nectar but many others feed on insects. A few, such as thrushes and starlings, eat just about anything, from insects and worms to larger prey and most members of the crow family are fierce predators that will attack small mammals and other birds.

Family	Corvidae
Latin name	*Pica pica*
Length	18½ in (47 cm)
Distribution	North America, Europe, North Africa, Asia

Black-billed magpie

Black-billed magpie

Also known as the common magpie, this bold, lively bird caches insects, snails, and slugs but also steals young from the nests of game birds and preys on rats and mice. A magpie can kill these creatures with a swift peck to the head. It also attacks smaller songbirds in the air, driving them down to the ground in order to kill and eat them. When food is plentiful, the magpie may hide food and it also feeds on carrion.

Rook

Like other members of the crow family, the rook is a noisy aggressive bird, but very intelligent. It eats almost anything and is always ready to take new foods and steal from other birds. It feeds on insects and worms, which it catches by driving its strong beak into the earth and forcing it open to seize the worm. It will also kill young birds and small mammals when it gets the chance.

Family	Corvidae
Latin name	*Corvus frugilegus*
Length	18 in (46 cm)
Distribution	Europe, Middle East, and Asia

Black butcherbird

The black butcherbird is a bold bird with a heavy hooked beak. It feeds mostly on the ground, where it hops around on its short legs. It preys on large insects, particularly grasshoppers, and small animals, such as lizards, and tears up anything that is too large to be swallowed whole. This bird lives alone or in small family groups.

Black butcherbird

Family	Cracticidae
Latin name	*Cracticus quoyi*
Length	12½–14¼ in (32–36 cm)
Distribution	Southeast Asia, New Guinea, Australia

Blackbird

The blackbird is a familiar garden bird. It eats a wide range of food, including insects and earthworms. It hunts mainly on the ground, watching out for prey and listening for any movement and is expert at pulling worms from the soil. It also hunts frogs and lizards.

Family	Turdidae
Latin name	*Turdus merula*
Length	10 in (25 cm)
Distribution	Europe, parts of Asia, and Australia

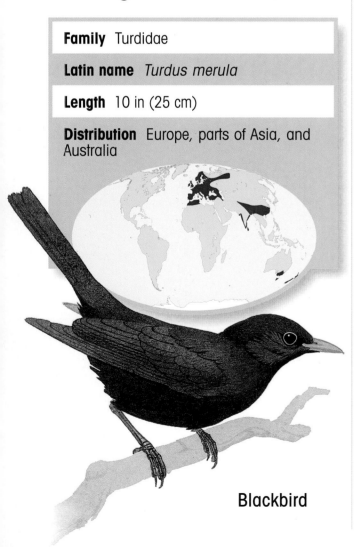

Blackbird

Great gray shrike

The 30 species of shrikes are all predatory songbirds. The great gray shrike finds a perch in a prominent position and flies out from there to capture prey on or near the ground. Insects are its main food but it also catches birds and mammals. Normally the bird returns to its perch to eat its catch, but it sometimes kills more than it needs and stores food, impaling the creature on thorns or barbed wire. It defends its territory fiercely against any intruders.

Family	Laniidae
Latin name	*Lanius excubitor*
Length	9½ in (24 cm)
Distribution	North America, Europe, North Africa, Asia

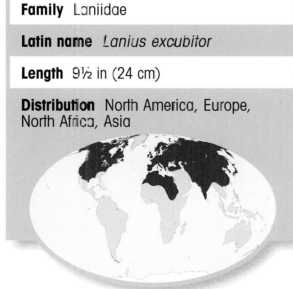

Great gray shrike

Insect-eating birds

Insects are the main food of many birds and they have a variety of ways of catching their prey. Even birds that generally eat seeds as adults, such as finches, may feed their young with insects so that they have enough protein to help them grow. Typical insect-eaters are warblers, which have small sharp beaks for getting insects out of cracks in tree bark and other crevices. Others, such as jacamars and flycatchers, have long pointed beaks for snapping up insects in the air. Nightingales usually find their insect prey on the ground.

Above Antshrikes perch on low branches watching for any insects that are disturbed by army ants.

Catching food for young

Many songbirds, including tits or chickadees, eat insects and spiders. These little birds hop around on bushes and trees, examining every leaf for insects and larvae. The busiest time for these birds is when they are rearing their young. The blue tit, for example, feeds its chicks mainly on caterpillars and must catch hundreds every day. This blue tit is flying back to its nest with a caterpillar in its beak.

Hunting techniques

Many birds catch insects in the air. Swifts are among the most expert fliers of all birds and rarely come to land. They catch insects in mid-flight and eat them in the air, too. Bee-eaters, flycatchers, and motmots, however, usually perch on branches and watch for insects to fly by. They then dart out to seize their prey in midair. As the bee-eater's name suggests, bees are its favorite food. Before eating the bee, the bird bangs or wipes the insect on a hard surface to remove the sting. The nightjar hunts at night and darts around after moths and other nocturnal insects. It flies with its beak open wide to scoop up its prey. Its beak is fringed with bristles that help trap insects.

The woodpecker has a different method. It has a very strong pointed beak, which it uses to hammer into tree bark to get at the earwigs and other creatures crawling underneath. Once it has made a hole in the bark, the woodpecker removes the insects with its long, sticky-tipped tongue, which it can stretch out well beyond the tip of its beak.

Antbirds have their own special way of finding insect prey. They watch for the insects fleeing from the huge troops of army ants that march across the forest floor. The antbird flutters from one low perch to another, keeping ahead of the column of ants. When it sees its chance, the bird darts down to snatch an insect or spider that was disturbed by the ants, then bounces back up to its perch. The antbird will also hop about among the ants to steal their prey. Its long legs help keep its body safe from stings and it also holds its tail up in the air.

Right Bee-eaters usually take their prey back to their perch before eating. This bee-eater has caught a dragonfly.

Reptiles are vertebrate animals, which evolved from amphibians about 300 million years ago. In the form of dinosaurs, reptiles were the dominant animals on Earth for more than 130 million years. At that time, as there are now, there were predatory as well as plant-eating reptiles.

Reptiles today

Four groups of reptiles survive today. Turtles and tortoises have short broad bodies enclosed by a shell into which the head, tail, and legs can be pulled for protection. The second group, which includes crocodiles and alligators, are the only remaining representatives of the group to which dinosaurs belonged—they are also the largest living reptiles. The third group includes lizards and snakes, and the fourth contains only the two species of tuataras, which live in New Zealand.

There are nearly 9,000 species of reptiles and they live all over the world, except in Antarctica.

They are, however, more common in warmer areas because they are cold-blooded—they cannot regulate their own body temperature like mammals and birds can and so they must rely on the sun for warmth. Most reptiles live on land, but there are marine turtles, some sea-living snakes, and one marine lizard.

Predatory reptiles

Except for some plant-eating tortoises and lizards, virtually all reptiles are predators. Snakes are some of the most efficient killers of all despite having no legs to use for attacking or holding prey. Boas wrap their victims in the coils of their body and tighten their grip until the prey can no longer breathe. Other snakes, such as vipers, kill with a poisonous bite.

Most lizards feed on small prey, such as insects, but the large species, such as the monitors, can catch animals as large as pigs and deer. Crocodiles and alligators are the top reptile predators. All hunt other animals, usually just by lying in wait for prey and taking the animal by surprise.

Above Like many snakes, the emerald tree boa has extremely flexible jaws, which it can open wide to eat prey larger than its own head.

Crocodiles

All 23 species in the crocodile family, which includes alligators, caimans, and the gharial as well as crocodiles, are powerful predators, which hunt a wide range of vertebrate animals. All have a long body, protected by thickened bony plates, and short legs. Both crocodiles and alligators have a pair of large teeth near the front of the jaw for grasping prey. In alligators, these teeth fit into bony pits in the upper jaw when the jaw is closed, but in crocodiles, they sit in notches on the outside of the upper jaw and remain visible.

West African
dwarf crocodile

Saltwater crocodile

This is the largest of the crocodiles and is a very dangerous animal. It generally hunts by lurking in the water, with only the top of its head visible above the surface as it watches for prey, such as buffalo or wild boar, to come to the water's edge to drink. The crocodile then makes a sudden lunge from the water, seizes its victim and drags it under the water until it drowns.

Family	Crocodylidae
Latin name	*Crocodylus porosus*
Length	16–23 ft (4.8–7 m)
Distribution	Southeast Asia, northern Australia

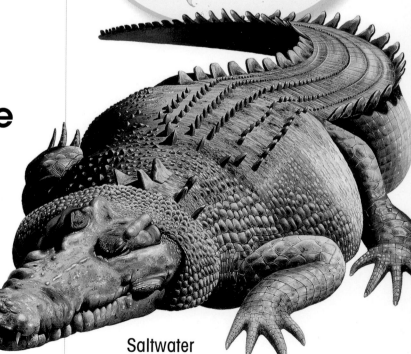

Saltwater
crocodile

West African dwarf crocodile

Family	Crocodylidae
Latin name	*Osteolaemus tetraspis*
Length	5½–6¼ ft (1.7–1.9 m)
Distribution	West Africa

Although this is the smallest of the crocodiles and has a short snout, it is still an efficient hunter and preys on fish, frogs, and other water creatures. It is generally active at night and spends the day in a burrow dug out near the water.

American alligator

With its strong jaws and up to 80 sharp teeth, the American alligator can tackle almost any prey that comes its way, including fish, turtles, small mammals, and birds. Like all crocodiles, the alligator cannot chew. When it catches prey too large to swallow whole, the alligator holds on to the prey in the water and spins its own body around to twist off chunks of flesh.

Family	Crocodylidae
Latin name	*Alligator mississippiensis*
Length	9¼–16 ft (2.8–4.8 m)
Distribution	Southeastern North America

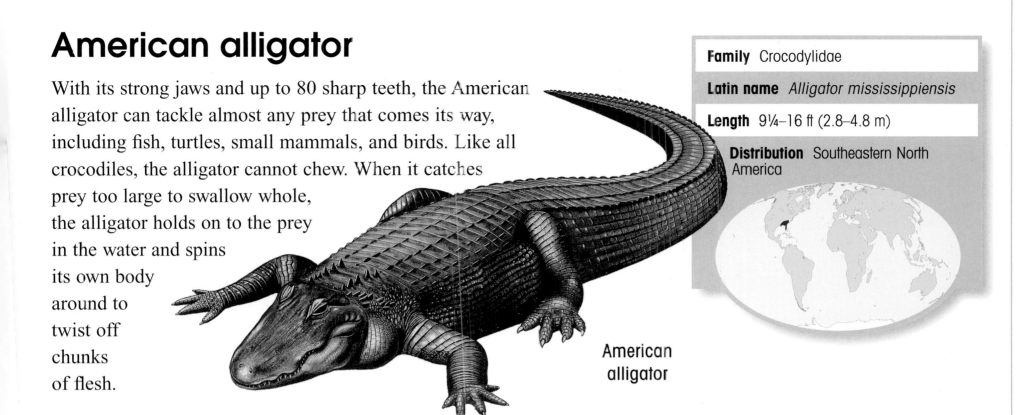

American alligator

Spectacled caiman

Family	Crocodylidae
Latin name	*Caiman crocodilus*
Length	6½–8 ft (2–2.4 m)
Distribution	Central and northern South America

Young caimans, like the young of other crocodiles and alligators, snap up small prey, such as insects and other small invertebrates. As they grow, they tackle larger and larger prey and more vertebrates. Full-grown caimans attack wild pigs and other large animals.

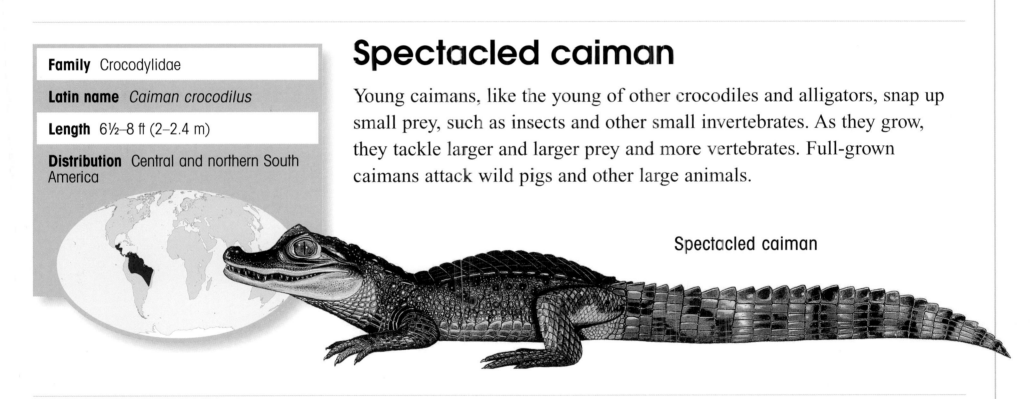

Spectacled caiman

Gharial

The gharial has a much longer and thinner snout than other crocodiles and this is an adaptation for its life as a fish-eater. The shape of the jaws means there is little resistance in the water as the gharial snaps for prey, and it also has 100 or so sharp teeth for holding on to struggling fish. The gharial spends most of its life in water and moves more awkwardly on land than other crocodiles.

Family	Crocodylidae
Latin name	*Gavialis gangeticus*
Length	13–23 ft (4–7 m)
Distribution	Northern India

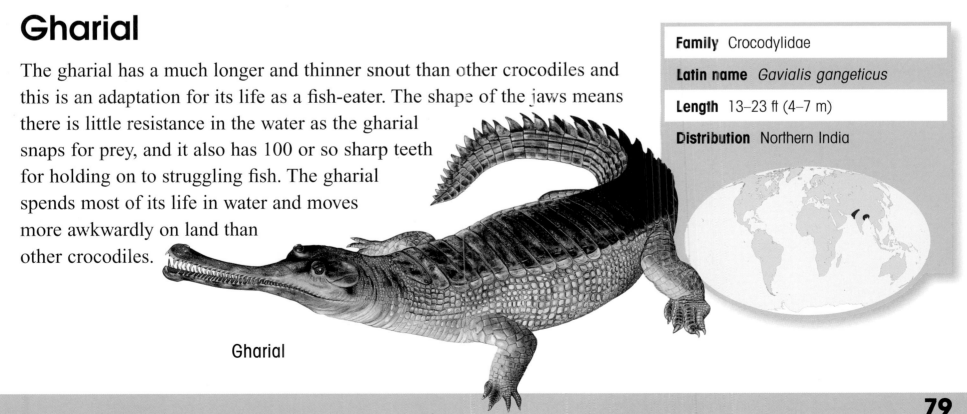

Gharial

How crocodiles hunt

Picture the scene. A group of wildebeests comes to a water hole to drink. All seems calm but near the group lies a crocodile almost submerged in the water so it is very hard to see. All of a sudden, the crocodile makes its attack.

Left The American crocodile has deadly teeth and powerful jaws and can grow up to 20 ft (6.1 m) long.

Drowning the victim

Just before the crocodile starts its dramatic lunge from the water, it often dives beneath the surface so even if the prey does spot its movement, the animal does not know where it is going to pop up. The crocodile then hurls itself toward the riverbank where, if it is lucky, it will manage to grab a victim by its leg, head, or tail. Once it has the prey in its grasp, the crocodile pulls the animal back into the water where it holds the struggling creature under the surface until the victim drowns.

Stealthy alligator

The American alligator spends most of its life in water, only emerging to bask in the sun from time to time. It is almost invisible as it lies at the water's surface with only its eyes and nose peeking above the water as it watches for prey. When necessary, it can slide through the water while hardly making a ripple as it creeps up on animals, such as a turtle resting on a log or a rat on the riverbank. It also feeds on fish, birds, carrion, and any other food it can find.

Above A group of wildebeests turn in alarm as a Nile crocodile lunges out of the water toward them.

81

Iguanas, agamids, and geckos

These are all large families of lizards—there are 600 or so species of iguanas, 300 of agamids, and more than 1,000 geckos. All geckos and most agamids and iguanas hunt other creatures, such as insects, to eat.

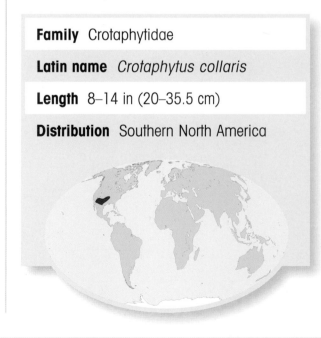

Collared lizard

Thorny devil

True to its name, this agamid lizard is covered with prickly spines, which protect it from predators. The devil eats ants and termites and can gobble up as many as 3,000 tiny ants in one session. It feeds by scooping up the insects one at a time with its long flicking tongue.

Family	Agamidae
Latin name	*Moloch horridus*
Length	6–7 in (15–18 cm)
Distribution	West and central Australia

Collared lizard

This lizard is a type of iguana. It is an agile fast-moving hunter and can run upright on two legs. It does catch insects but its main victims are other lizards, which it catches in its large jaws. It hunts during the day when it runs around rocks, looking for unwary lizards basking in the sun.

Family	Crotaphytidae
Latin name	*Crotaphytus collaris*
Length	8–14 in (20–35.5 cm)
Distribution	Southern North America

Thorny devil

Berthold's bush anole

This tree-living iguanid hunts by stealth. It lies on a branch, its flattened body pressed against the surface so it is hard to see as it lies in wait for insect prey. It is a good climber and is able to hold on to a branch with its back legs alone, but it is slow-moving.

Family	Iguanidae
Latin name	*Polychrus gutturosus*
Length	Up to 19¾ in (50 cm)
Distribution	Central and northern South America

Berthold's bush anole

Family	Gekkonidae
Latin name	*Gekko gecko*
Length	7–14 in (18–35.5 cm)
Distribution	Southeast Asia

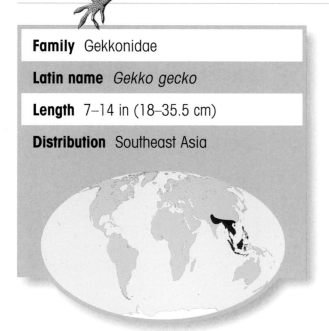

Tokay gecko

One of the largest and fiercest geckos, the tokay lives in trees in tropical rain forests. It hunts insects, such as cockroaches, as well as smaller lizards, mice, and young birds and snaps up its prey in its strong jaws. It lives alone and defends its territory against other geckos so there is less competition for food. Like many geckos, it has specialized scales under its toes that enable it to climb easily up vertical surfaces.

Tokay gecko

Leopard gecko

This brightly patterned gecko hides away during the day and comes out at night to hunt insects, such as grasshoppers and beetles, as well as spiders and scorpions. Its chunky tail is used to store fat when food is plentiful. This helps the gecko survive through periods of drought or food shortage. However, if grabbed by a predator, the gecko may shed its tail—and lose its store of fat.

Family	Gekkonidae
Latin name	*Eublepharis macularius*
Length	8–10 in (20–25 cm)
Distribution	South Asia

Leopard gecko

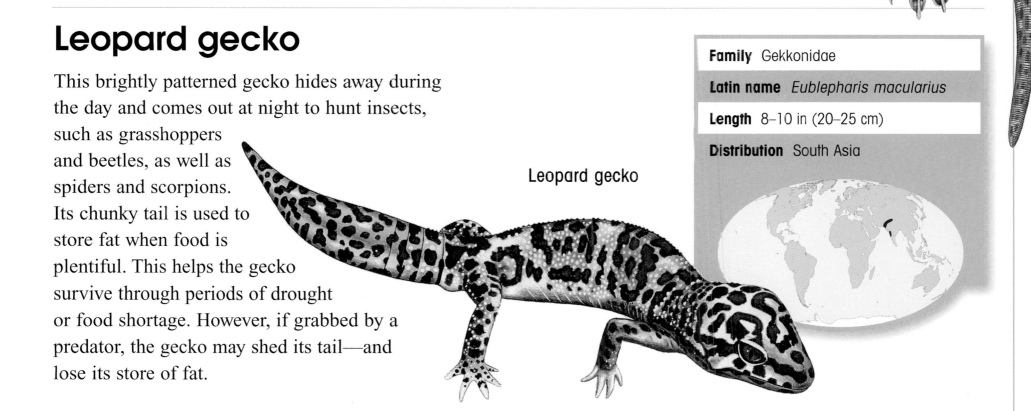

Chameleons

With a tongue like moving fly-paper, the chameleon is perfectly equipped for preying on insects. Chameleons are a kind of lizard. There are at least 175 species, most of which live in Africa and Madagascar. There is one European chameleon.

Above The tiniest chameleons are only about an inch (2.5 cm) long, but they still hunt for their prey with a lightning-fast strike of the tongue.

Patient hunters

Chameleons are not fast runners. They hunt by staying very still on the branch of a tree and waiting for an insect to come near enough to catch. Each foot is adapted for holding branches, with two clawed toes on one side and three on the other. The tail is prehensile and can also be used for gripping. The tail helps to keep the chameleon steady as it catches its prey. A chameleon's eyes can move independently so it can see all around itself without moving. But when the chameleon spots prey, it focuses both eyes on the victim and takes aim.

Above This short-horned chameleon lives in forests in Madagascar. It has just succeeded in catching an insect on the sticky pad at the end of its tongue. In a split second, the insect will be in the chameleon's mouth.

Insects are their main prey, but large chameleons sometimes catch small birds. The chameleon catches its prey with its tongue, which can be as long as its body. This gives the reptile a long reach so it does not have to get too close to its prey. Chameleons also rely on staying hidden so their victims do not see them first. They cannot turn any color they feel like, but most have a range of colors that they are able to adopt. Chameleons also change color in the breeding season and when afraid or angry.

Right Like all chameleons, the panther chameleon has ridges on the underside of its feet to help it grip.

How the chameleon's tongue works

The tongue is operated by muscles. When the chameleon is ready to strike, these muscles shoot the tongue forward and out of the chameleon's mouth in a fraction of a second. The prey is caught on a pad, covered with sticky saliva, at the end of the long tongue, and is back in the chameleon's mouth before the creature has time to react.

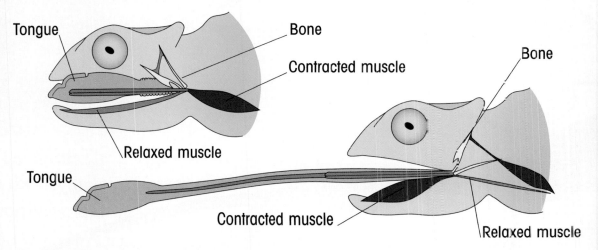

Tongue
Bone
Contracted muscle
Relaxed muscle
Tongue
Contracted muscle
Bone
Relaxed muscle

Above The chameleon's tongue can be shot out at speeds of up to 16 ft (4.8 m) a second.

Snakes—special senses

Like all vertebrate animals, snakes experience their surroundings and find the food they need by using their senses. Most snakes have very well developed senses—and some, such as the pit vipers and some pythons and boas, have an extra-special sense that enables them to hunt in complete darkness.

Above Because a snake's tongue is forked, it can cover a wide area and gather more chemical clues. This snake is a painted bronzeback, which lives in Southeast Asia.

Taste, smell, and hearing

As a snake moves around, it constantly flicks its forked tongue in and out of its mouth. As it does so, it collects tiny particles from the ground and air. These are carried back into the snake's mouth to a special structure in the roof of the mouth called the Jacobson's organ. This organ is lined with sensitive cells that help the snake analyze the particles it has gathered and so helps it track its prey. The snake is "tasting" what is going on around it. Snakes also have a sense of smell like humans do and they have small external nostrils, which are near the tip of the nose.

Snakes do not have any external ear openings and because of this, it used to be thought that they could not hear. Scientists have now discovered that snakes can, in fact, hear some sounds.

Right One of the eyelash viper's heat-sensitive pits can be clearly seen between its eye and nostril. This pit viper lives in South America.

They hear by simply resting the jaw on the ground and picking up the vibrations. These vibrations are then analyzed by the inner ear, which also helps to control the snake's balance, just as it does in humans. Snakes are sensitive to touch, too, and their skin responds to pressure and to heat.

Heat-sensors

Most amazing of all snake senses are the heat-sensing abilities of some species that allow them to find prey at night. In the pit vipers, the heat-sensing pits are located on each side of the snake's head, between the eye and the nostril. These organs can pick up tiny differences in temperature, enabling the snake to "see" the heat generated by warm-blooded prey, such as rats. The snake may not be able to see the rat with its eyes, but the "heat picture" allows it to strike its prey accurately.

Snake eyes

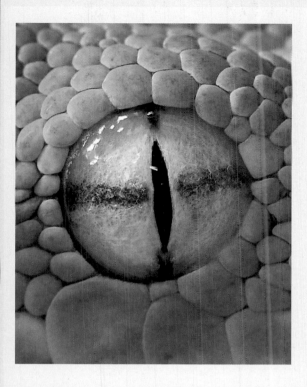

A snake may look like it is always staring because it does not have moveable eyelids as humans do. Instead, a snake's eye is covered with a transparent scale that is shed and renewed each time the snake sheds its skin. How well a snake sees varies from group to group. Some burrowing snakes are only able to tell light from dark, but others that hunt on land or in trees can see well, particularly anything that is moving.

Above Like most snakes that are active at night, this python has eyes with vertical pupils that can open up in dim light.

Turtles and tortoises

There are nearly 300 species of turtles and tortoises living all over the world and while many are plant-eaters, some hunt other creatures. They do not have teeth and cannot move fast so they tend to prey on slow-moving creatures, such as snails, worms, and slugs. A typical turtle or tortoise has a hard shell made of bony plates and horn that protects the body.

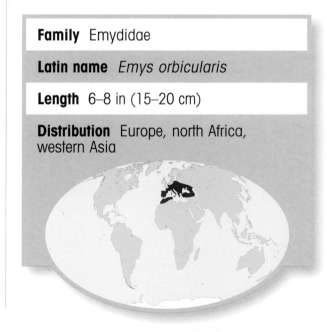

European pond turtle

Narrow-headed softshell

A fast-moving turtle with flipperlike limbs, the softshell is well adapted for life in water. It finds most of its food in water and preys on creatures, such as fish, shrimp, and snails, which it snatches in its hard toothless beak.

Family	Trionychidae
Latin name	*Chitra indica*
Length	35 ½–45 in (90–114 cm)
Distribution	India, Pakistan, Nepal

European pond turtle

This is one of the few freshwater turtles in Europe. It spends most of its time in slow-moving water but does come out onto land to sun itself during the day. It is carnivorous and feeds on fish, frogs, snails, and worms, which it hunts in water and on land. In winter, this turtle hibernates for up to seven months in mud or in a burrow dug into a riverbank.

Family	Emydidae
Latin name	*Emys orbicularis*
Length	6–8 in (15–20 cm)
Distribution	Europe, north Africa, western Asia

Narrow-headed softshell

Matamata

The strange-looking matamata turtle hunts by stealth and stays hidden so it can surprise its prey. With its leaflike head and rough, ridged shell it looks like a pile of bark and leaves as it lies at the bottom of the river watching for prey. Its hunting method is very simple—when prey comes near, the matamata opens its mouth and water and creatures are sucked in.

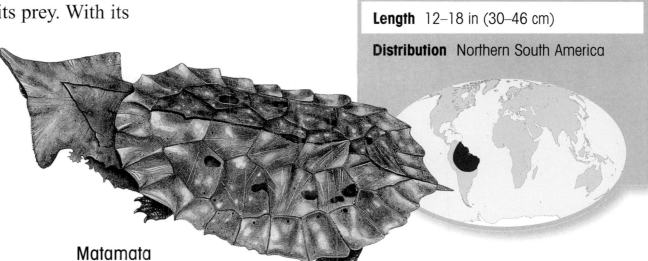

Family	Chelidae
Latin name	*Chelus fimbriatus*
Length	12–18 in (30–46 cm)
Distribution	Northern South America

Matamata

Loggerhead

This big sea-living turtle has a large head and very powerful jaws that it uses to crush hard-shelled prey, such as crabs, clams, and other mollusks. When migrating to breeding beaches and traveling through open sea, the loggerhead also eats jellyfish and squid. Young turtles feed mostly on sponges and jellyfish.

Family	Cheloniidae
Latin name	*Caretta caretta*
Length	33½–48½ in (85–123 cm)
Distribution	Atlantic, Pacific, and Indian oceans

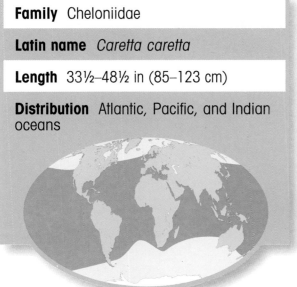

Alligator snapping turtle

This turtle is the largest freshwater turtle in North America. It moves so little that algae grows on its back and helps camouflage it as it lies in wait for prey on the riverbed. To hunt, it opens its huge jaws showing the little pink fleshy flap that hangs from the mouth. Fish come to investigate this, thinking it might be a tasty morsel of food and the turtle's strong jaws then snap shut, trapping the prey. The turtle also eats crustaceans.

Family	Chelydridae
Latin name	*Macroclemys temminckii*
Length	16–32 in (41–81 cm)
Distribution	Southeast U.S.A.

Alligator snapping turtle

Amphibians

There are nearly 6,000 species of amphibians living all over the world. They are divided into three main groups—frogs and toads, newts and salamanders, and the limbless, burrowing creatures known as caecilians. Their skin is smooth, not scaly, but must stay moist. Adult amphibians do have lungs, but they also breathe in air through their skin.

The first vertebrates

Amphibians were the first vertebrate animals to live on land. They evolved from fish more than 350 million years ago and most amphibians still spend at least part of their lives in water.

Most amphibians also lay their eggs in water. The eggs hatch into aquatic tadpoles, which have fins and gills. As the tadpoles grow, they develop legs and lungs so they can survive on land. Although many frog and toad tadpoles feed on plants,

all adult amphibians are carnivores and feed on a variety of prey—mostly insects and other small invertebrates.

Best of two worlds

By spending the first part of its life as a tadpole, a frog or salamander gets the best of two worlds. A tadpole is fully equipped for underwater life, with a tail to power its swimming and gills that enable it to breathe underwater. As it grows, the tadpole begins to breathe air through its lungs and moist skin. When fully grown, it is able to live at

least partly on land. So for both of the two very different phases of its life, the frog or salamander has a body suited to its activities. Because the tadpole and adult lead such different lives, they do not compete with each other for space or food.

Many amphibians have very brightly colored and patterned skin. This is a warning to potential predators that the skin contains nasty-tasting secretions, which can cause severe irritation. Some frogs, such as the poison-dart frogs, contain venom that is so strong it can even kill mammals.

Below Two edible frogs battle with each other for a large juicy earthworm, which is one of their favorite types of prey.

A swimming pincushion

The porcupine pufferfish cannot swim fast, but it has a very special way of protecting itself. If threatened or attacked by a predator, it puffs its body up with water until it is about twice its normal size. When inflated like this, the spines on its body, which normally lie flat, stick straight out and make the fish look like a swimming pincushion. Once the danger has past, the pufferfish returns to its normal shape and size.

Above When fully inflated, the pufferfish is safe from all but the largest or most determined predators.

Staying safe

Life for many animals is a constant battle between finding their own food and avoiding being eaten by other creatures. Animals from all groups have ways of staying safe, such as camouflage, spines, or warning colors, which do not require any additional action. All these strategies help them avoid predators. The predators learn from experience that a snake with bright red stripes is poisonous, or that a hedgehog's spines can be painful.

Above The poison-dart frog's brightly colored skin warns of the poisonous secretions it contains.

Camouflage

Good camouflage can make animals very hard for predators to see by helping them blend in with their surroundings. Many insects are colored or even shaped to look like the leaves they live among. Some insects have irregular edges to their wings, making them look like leaves that have been nibbled by hungry caterpillars. A stick insect can be difficult to tell from a real twig and there are moths that are colored like lichen-covered bark.

Left The wings of this giant leaf katydid are not only shaped like leaves but have veinlike markings.

Some creatures go to the other extreme and try to escape predators by being very brightly colored—for example, a wasp's bold stripes warn that it stings. Many kinds of frogs, snakes, and lizards also have bright markings or coloration, which usually signals that they have poisonous secretions in their skin or a venomous bite.

The coral snake's black and red stripes warn of its deadly bite. Amazingly, there are other snakes that have very similar coloration though they are not poisonous—they gain protection from looking like the coral snake.

Another means of self-defense is a coat of prickly spines or strong body armor. An armadillo's body is protected by tough plates made of bone and covered by horn. If attacked, the armadillo rolls up into a tight ball making it very hard for anything to attack. A porcupine is covered with up to 30,000 sharp quills, or spines—if necessary, it will drive these quills into a predator.

Fish

Fish were the first of the vertebrate animals and the earliest known lived about 500 million years ago. Now there are more fish than any other kind of vertebrate animal—at least 24,500 species are known and there are believed to be many more that are still undiscovered. They range from tiny creatures, such as the pygmy goby, which is only about ½ in (1 cm) long, to the huge whale shark, which measures more than 39 ft (12 m) long.

All fish live in water. At least 14,000 species live in the sea and the rest in freshwater rivers and lakes. A few kinds of fish, such as salmon, move between freshwater and the sea. Fish breathe by using special structures called gills on the sides of the head. As water flows through the gills, oxygen passes into the blood and is then carried around the body. Instead of legs, fish have fins and a tail to help them move through water.

Right A great white shark bursts through the water's surface, displaying its huge jaws and terrifying teeth.

Main types of fish

There are three main groups of fish. Most primitive are the lampreys and hagfish. These animals have no jaws, only a suckerlike mouth. The second group includes all the sharks and rays and these are known as cartilaginous fish because their skeletons are made of a gristly substance called cartilage, not bone. The third and largest group contains the bony fish, which have skeletons made of bone.

How fish feed

Some fish feed entirely on aquatic plants but others hunt for their food. Many catch tiny animals or strain them from the water through filterlike structures attached to their gills. Some, such as sharks, tuna, and swordfish, are active, fast-moving hunters with sharp teeth, while others, such as flatfish and anglerfish, simply lie on the seabed waiting for prey to come close enough to snap up.

Fighting back

While many creatures try to stay out of sight of their enemies or run away if threatened, others have much more active ways of defending themselves. Many kinds of insects, as well as sea creatures, such as jellyfish, bite or sting their attackers. The bombardier beetle is fiercer still. It sprays boiling-hot chemicals out of its abdomen at any predator that dares to come too close.

Above If a predator threatens her nest, the killdeer tries to lead it away by pretending she has a broken wing.

Spraying blood

The horned lizard is a spiny reptile with a rounded body. It feeds on large amounts of ants. It is not a fast mover and spends much of its time sitting by the nests of its prey. But if a predator, such as a coyote, dares to attack it, this lizard has an extraordinary way of protecting itself—it sprays its enemy with a bloody liquid from its eyes. Amazingly, this blood contains formic acid, which comes from the lizard's diet of ants. This acid irritates the attacker's eyes and mouth and so the animal soon gives up and goes away.

Tricks and tactics

Skunks also spray their enemies—they spray a smelly, oily liquid from glands under the tail. The spray does not do any real damage but it confuses the predator, giving the skunk a chance to escape. A seabird called the fulmar has a similar technique—it spits a foul-smelling oil at anything that tries to steal its eggs or young. Terns gang up and dive-bomb any intruders into their nests. Musk oxen also gather together to protect their young. If threatened by a predator, the oxen form a ring with their young in the center.

Other animals try tricks. Toads puff themselves up with air to look bigger than they really are. Butterflies flash markings that look like giant eyes on their wings—these give the impression that the butterfly might be a much larger creature that would be difficult to catch. Some birds try to distract any predator that approaches their nest. The killdeer, for example, moves away from her nest, dragging her wing as if she is injured. The predator follows thinking that she is an easy victim and then the bird suddenly flies up and escapes.

Right The bad-smelling spray produced by a skunk can travel 10 ft (3 m) or more and can stink for days.

Deep-sea hunters

The deep sea is one of the most mysterious places on earth: The surface waters of the ocean are brightly lit by the sun's rays, but from about 650 ft (200 m) deep, the light begins to decrease and below 3,300 ft (1,000 m), the ocean is completely dark. Plants need light and so they cannot grow in the deep sea. This means that all deep-sea creatures are predators and must survive by hunting each other or scavenging on any dead animals and other debris that sink down from the waters above. The deep sea is cold too—about 35–39°F (2–4°C) in most places.

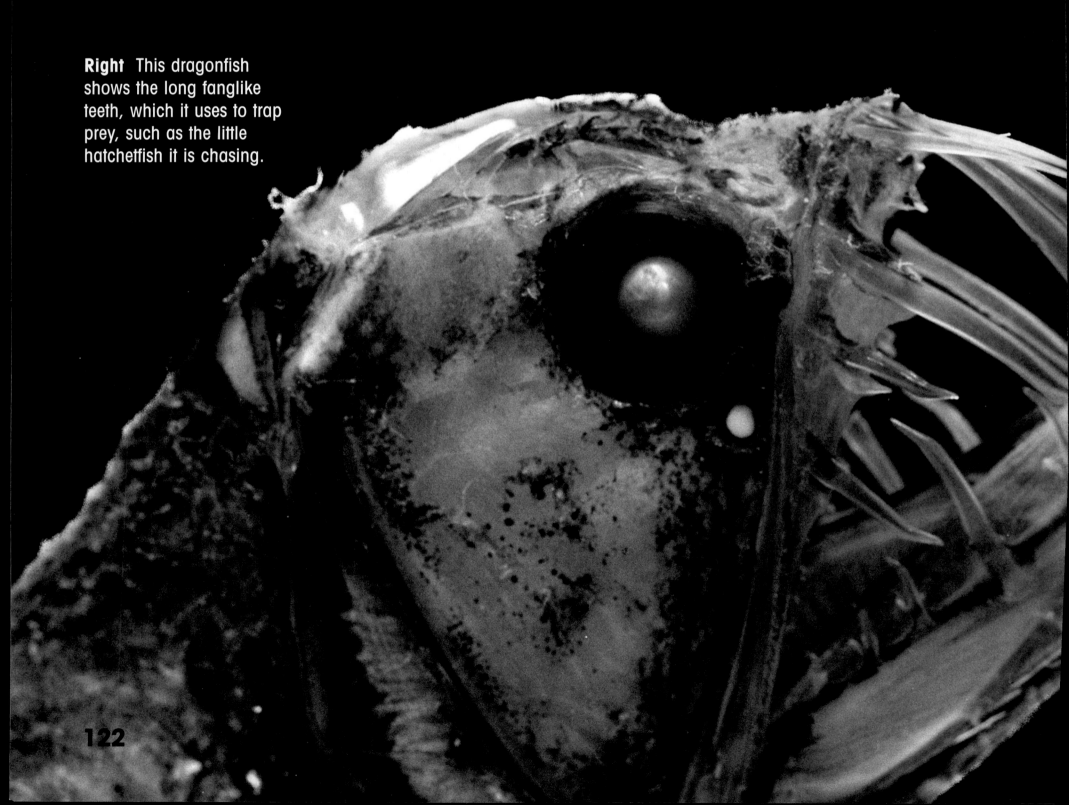

Right This dragonfish shows the long fanglike teeth, which it uses to trap prey, such as the little hatchetfish it is chasing.

Light in the darkness

In these difficult conditions, deep-sea creatures have had to develop special ways of finding enough food to eat. Many deep-sea fish have long sharp teeth and large mouths for their size so they can take advantage of any prey that happens to pass by. Deep-sea shrimp have extra-long antennae, which they spread out in the water to pick up the slightest movement and find prey.

Most deep-sea creatures solve the problem of the darkness by carrying their own sources of light. Special light-producing organs are arranged in rows on the body and light is made by chemical reactions inside these organs. The lights can help a fish find food in the darkness.

The lights may also confuse other predators and can help fish find mates. Some, such as the football fish and the viperfish, also have a kind of luminous lure that they use as a fishing rod to catch prey. The lure is tipped with a light-producing organ that attracts other fish that are looking for food. As they come close to investigate, they are snapped up by the predator.

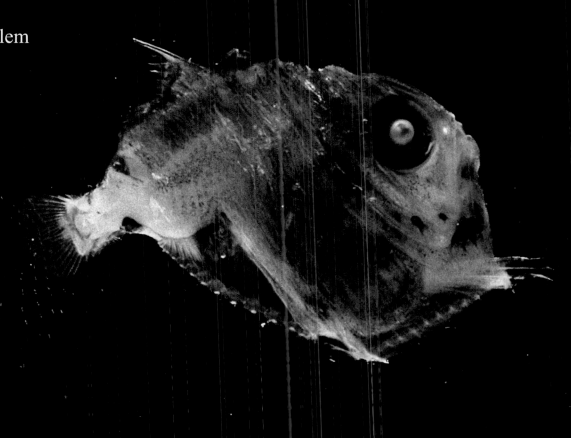

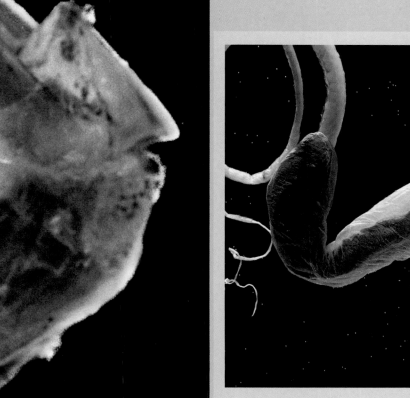

Deep-sea gulper

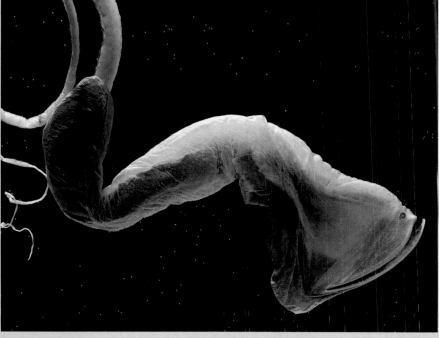

True to its name, the gulper has huge gaping jaws that seem too big for its slender body. This large mouth means that the eel can swallow prey that is up to twice its own size and its slender tubelike body can stretch to hold large meals. It also has a light-producing organ at the tip of its tail. It feeds mostly on crustaceans but also eats fish and squid. The gulper usually lives at depths of 6,550–10,000 ft (2,000–3,000 m).

Above The gulper can grow to more than 6 ft (1.8 m) long. Its hinged jaws swing wide open to engulf prey.

Right The tiger beetle's huge serrated jaws are powerful tools for cutting up and chewing prey.

Insects and other invertebrates

Insects are invertebrate animals—they do not have backbones. In terms of numbers, they are the most successful creatures on Earth. There are at least a million species and probably more still to be discovered. Most insects are small at less than an inch (2.5 cm) long, and they live in nearly every type of habitat. Creatures, such as flies, beetles, butterflies, and dragonflies are all insects.

A typical insect

An insect's body has three parts—head, thorax, and abdomen. The head carries the eyes, mouthparts, and a pair of sensory antennae, which the insect uses to find out about its surroundings. The mouthparts may be adapted for chewing food or for sucking or lapping up liquids. On the thorax are the insect's three pairs of legs and, usually, two pairs of wings. The abdomen houses the reproductive organs and most of the digestive system. A tough waterproof layer outside the body protects the insect.

Insects eat an amazing range of different foods. Some feed on plants, including dead wood and rotting plant material, but others, such as many kinds of beetles, flies, and wasps, are hunters.

Other invertebrates

Spiders and scorpions are not insects— they belong to a separate group of invertebrates called arachnids. Typically, a spider's body is divided into two parts and it has four pairs of legs. All spiders and scorpions live by hunting other creatures and some have venomous bites. Many spiders catch their prey in webs woven from silk spun from their own body.

There are also many other types of invertebrates. On land, there are creatures, such as worms, snails, and centipedes. In the sea, there is an amazing range of invertebrate life, such as lobsters, crabs, octopuses, and jellyfish. Many of these animals live by preying on other creatures.

Left This mantid is about to strike an unsuspecting grasshopper. The movement is so fast that it cannot be seen with the naked eye. One moment the prey is sitting on a leaf and the next it will be struggling in the mantid's jaws.

Traps and weapons

Insects may be small, but many are fierce hunters and have a range of techniques for trapping and killing their prey. Some, such as water bugs, simply seize prey in their powerful front legs and bite the victim with strong beaklike mouthparts. The robber fly catches its prey with its strong legs and then sucks out the victim's body fluids. Tiny ants can inflict painful bites, and bees and wasps all have a sharp sting at the end of the body. While wasps and hornets can pull their stings out of their victim and use them again, a bee can only use its sting once.

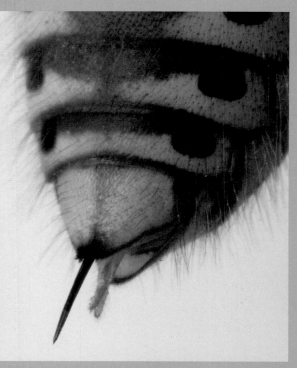

Above The sharp sting at the end of a hornet's body is linked to a bag of venom, which is injected into the prey.

The antlion's trap

This fierce little creature is the larva of an insect that looks like a dragonfly. The antlion digs a pit in sandy soil and waits at the bottom. If an insect strays near the edge of the pit, it slips down with the sliding sand and into the jaws of the waiting antlion.

Sting or strike

Bees use their stings to defend themselves, but wasps and hornets also sting to kill prey to feed to their young. Adult wasps feed mostly on nectar and other plant matter, such as ripe fruit. The sting is made up of a tube with two sharp points. As the insect pushes the sting into its victim, venom flows down through the tube and paralyzes the creature.

The praying mantis does not have a sting, but it is one of the most cunning and best equipped of all killer insects. Its front pair of legs are much larger than the others and have much stronger muscles. The inside edges of the front legs are also lined with sharp spines, which help the mantid hold its prey, however much the victim struggles. The hunting technique is simple. The mantid lies in wait, watching for prey. Unusually for an insect, the mantid can turn its head right around to look over its shoulder as it follows its prey's movements. Its widely spaced eyes help it pinpoint the position and take aim. When it is sure of its target, the mantid shoots out its front legs to seize the victim.

137

Flies

Flies are among the most common insects and with more than 124,000 species, make up one of the largest groups. Their most distinctive feature is that they have only one pair of wings, not two like butterflies and beetles. In some flies, the back wings have become small knobbed structures called halteres, which help the fly to balance as it flies. Many flies feed on nectar and plant sap, but some are predators and kill other insects to eat. Scorpionflies are not true flies and belong to a different group of about 550 species.

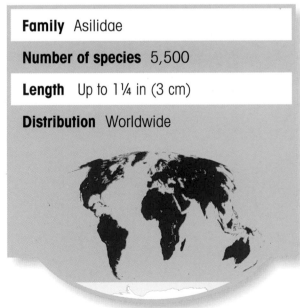

Robber fly and prey

Dance flies

These flies prey on smaller insects, but in the breeding season, male dance flies also catch prey to give to females. The male offers the female his gift to attract and distract her—the female is larger than the male and sometimes eats him before he can mate.

Family	Empididae
Number of species	4,000
Length	Up to ⅝ in (1.5 cm)
Distribution	Worldwide

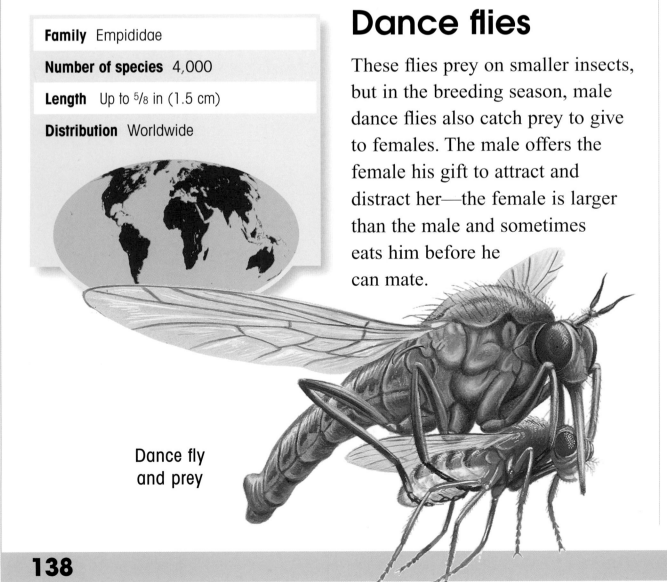

Dance fly and prey

Robber flies

Robber flies are fast-moving predators, which catch other insects, such as butterflies, in the air or on the ground. The fly seizes its prey in its strong bristly legs and holds the victim while it sucks out the creature's body fluids with its short, sharp mouthparts.

Family	Asilidae
Number of species	5,500
Length	Up to 1¼ in (3 cm)
Distribution	Worldwide

Dung fly

This predatory fly is often seen in fields where cows are grazing and lays its eggs in cow dung. The male fly stays near his mate while she lays eggs and defends the cow pie from other flies. The larvae feed on the dung but also eat other insects if they get the chance. As adults, dung flies prey on houseflies and other insects.

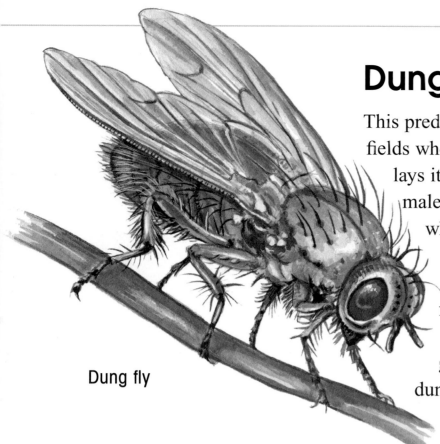
Dung fly

Family	Scathophagidae
Latin name	*Scatophaga stercoraria*
Length	Up to 3/8 in (1 cm)
Distribution	North America

Bee flies

Adult bee flies look very much like their namesake. Many feed as bees do and hover in front of flowers to collect nectar. Their larvae, however, are predators. The eggs are laid near the nest of another insect, such as a bee or beetle. When the larvae hatch, they make their way into the other insects' nest and feed on their larvae.

Family	Bombyliidae
Number of species	5,000
Length	Up to 5/8 in (1.5 cm)
Distribution	Worldwide

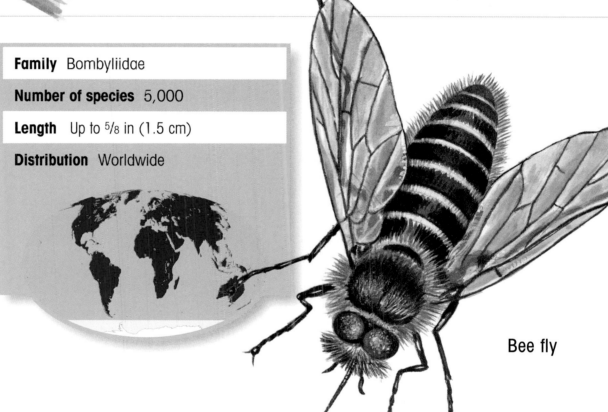
Bee fly

Hanging scorpionflies

These insects look a lot like large mosquitoes. They prey on other flying insects, which they catch by hanging upside down from twigs by their long front legs and grabbing the passing insects with their back legs. They also sometimes catch prey while in flight. Males offer a dead victim to females before mating. Scorpionfly larvae also feed mainly on dead insects.

Hanging scorpionfly

Family	Bittacidae
Number of species	About 170
Length	Up to 1 in (2.5 cm)
Distribution	Worldwide

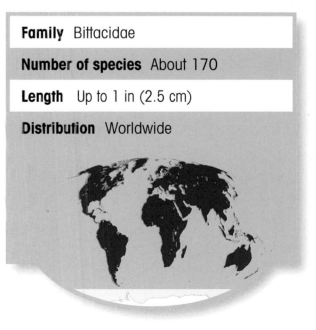

Beetles

With more than a quarter of a million species, beetles are the largest group of insects and some of the most successful of all living creatures. They live in almost every type of habitat, from polar areas to rain forests and the driest deserts, and range in size from tiny creatures that can barely be seen to the huge goliath beetles that are 4 in (10 cm) long. Typically, a beetle has two pairs of wings. The front wings are hard and thick and act as covers for the more delicate back wings when they are not in use for flight.

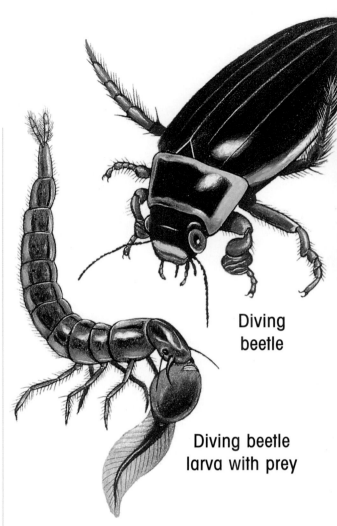

Diving beetle

Diving beetle larva with prey

Tiger beetles

Tiger beetles are fast-moving hunters, which prey on other insects, catching them in their big jaws. Their larvae are equally fierce, but they hunt by ambush. They lie in wait at the entrance to their burrow, waiting to grab any passing creatures, which they then pull into the burrow. Both adults and larvae chew up their food, and then liquefy it with a special digestive fluid.

Family	Cicindelidae
Number of species	More than 2,000
Length	Up to ¾ in (2 cm)
Distribution	Worldwide

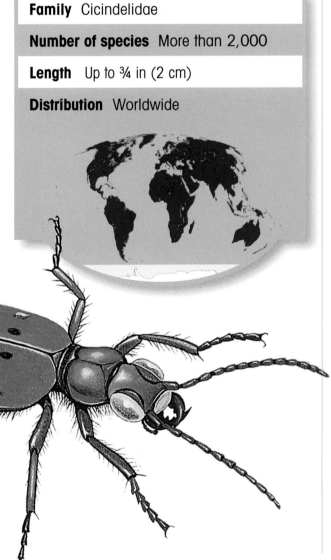

Tiger beetle

Diving beetles

Both adult diving beetles and their larvae are fierce predators, which live in water. The larvae, known as water tigers, have strong jaws and often attack prey larger than themselves. The adults prey on fish and other water creatures. They are strong swimmers and use their long, fringed back legs like oars to push themselves through the water.

Family	Dytiscidae
Number of species	More than 4,000
Length	Up to 1½ in (4 cm)
Distribution	Worldwide

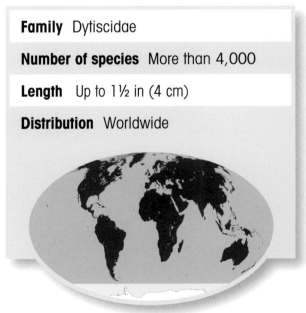

Caterpillar hunter

This beetle is also known as the "searcher" because it hunts down and kills caterpillars. Their larvae also eat caterpillars and both adults and larvae will climb trees to find their prey. These beetles give off an unpleasant smelling liquid if touched or attacked.

Family	Carabidae
Latin name	*Calosoma scrutator*
Length	¾–1¼ in (2–3 cm)
Distribution	North America

Caterpillar hunter

Ladybug beetles

Gardeners love ladybugs, as both adults and larvae feed on aphids, which can be serious plant pests. The ladybug's bright colors help protect it from other predators— they warn others that it tastes nasty and could be poisonous.

Family	Coccinellidae
Number of species	5,000
Length	Up to ³/₈ in (1 cm)
Distribution	Worldwide

Ladybug beetle

Rove beetles

These active little beetles run around with their long tail lifted, rather like scorpions. They hunt other insects, mites, and even worms, which they catch with their sharp jaws. This is one of the largest families of beetles and they are particularly common in tropical areas.

Rove beetle

Family	Staphylinidae
Number of species	At least 45,000
Length	Up to ¾ in (2 cm)
Distribution	Worldwide

Living on others— parasites and parasitic larvae

Not all animals that feed on others are big and fierce, like tigers and sharks. Some are tiny creatures that have a more underhand way of finding food—they are parasites. A parasite is any creature that lives in or on another creature (called a host). Parasites do not usually kill their host—if the host goes, so does the food supply.

Parasites

Parasites include fleas, which jump up onto warm-blooded animals, such as cats and dogs, to feed on their blood; tapeworms, which live in an animal's digestive system and absorb its food as they grow to lengths that can be 20 ft (6.1 m) or more; and ticks, which suck blood from their hosts. There are also parasites that live on humans. For example, there is a kind of louse that can cling to human skin or hairs with hooks on the end of its legs. The louse feeds on blood with its hollow, piercing mouthparts.

Left This wasp is laying its egg in an aphid. When the egg hatches, the young wasp will eat the aphid's body.

Insect killers

Still more deadly are the parasitoids. These are insects that lay their eggs in or on another animal. When the eggs hatch, the larvae tunnel their way into their host or start eating the creature from within. The host animal always dies, either from damage to its insides or from the wounds made as the larvae enter its body. Female braconid wasps, for example, insert their eggs into the larvae of other insects, which are often moth caterpillars. As soon as the larvae hatch, they start eating the caterpillar's body—from the inside. At a later stage, they make their way outside of the body to spin little cocoons in which they change into adults.

Blood feeder

Hard ticks do not actually kill, but they do feed on the blood of their host and can spread serious diseases, probably more than any other type of invertebrate. They attach themselves with their strong mouthparts and remain on their host for several days.

Above A group of braconid wasp young in their cocoons are attached to this caterpillar, which will soon die.

143

Scorpions and mites

Scorpions and their relatives are not insects but are arachnids, like spiders. There are true scorpions, wind scorpions, and whip scorpions, but only the true scorpions have a venomous bite. All are fierce hunters, however. Mites and ticks are the smallest of the arachnids, but there are at least 48,000 species of them and they live all over the world in every kind of habitat. Some mites hunt prey while others live as parasites. Ticks feed by sucking blood from host animals.

Buthid scorpion

Family	Buthidae
Number of species	528
Length	2–2¾ in (5–7 cm)
Distribution	Tropical and warm temperate areas worldwide

Wind scorpions

Wind scorpions are common in desert areas and are also known as sun spiders. They are fast runners and chase insects and other creatures, including small lizards, rodents, and snakes, which they catch in their large pincers. These pincers can be as much as a third of the scorpion's total length. A wind scorpion's bite is not venomous but it crushes its victim to a pulp with its sharp jaws and then covers it in a digestive fluid. This turns the flesh to liquid so the wind scorpion can suck it up.

Family	Eremobatidae
Number of species	187
Length	Up to 1¾ in (4.5 cm)
Distribution	North and Central America

Wind scorpion

Buthid scorpions

Armed with a venomous stinger at the end of the body and massive pincers for grasping prey, these scorpions are fierce hunters. When ready to attack, the scorpion swings its sting forward so it can plunge it into its victim to kill the creature. Scorpions are generally active at night and stay hidden during the day.

Whip scorpions

Whip scorpions have no sting, but catch prey, such as small insects and millipedes, with their large pincers. The whip scorpion's other common name is vinegaroon because it can spray an acidic, vinegary liquid from glands near the base of its tail when it is attacked or afraid.

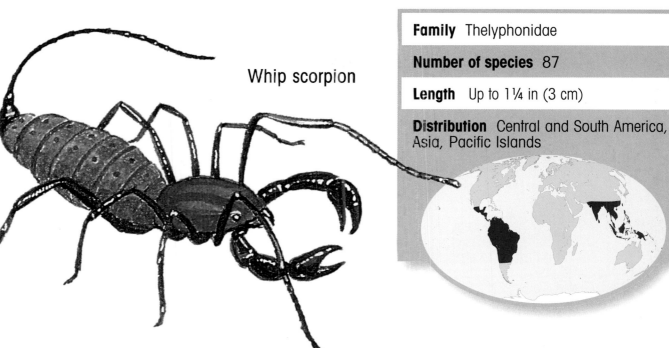

Whip scorpion

Family	Thelyphonidae
Number of species	87
Length	Up to 1¼ in (3 cm)
Distribution	Central and South America, Asia, Pacific Islands

Hard ticks

Hard ticks cannot jump or fly but can climb. They crawl onto the body of any animal and remain there, feeding on the animal's blood with their sucking mouthparts. As they feed, they may pass on deadly diseases, such as Lyme disease.

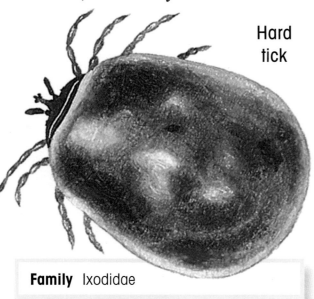

Hard tick

Family	Ixodidae
Number of species	650
Length	⅛ in (3 mm)
Distribution	Worldwide

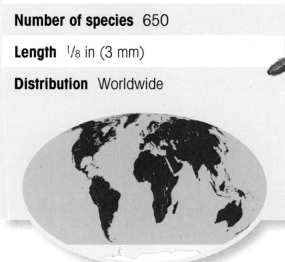

Velvet mites

These little mites are not fierce hunters but in their own way they help to keep insect numbers down. Adult velvet mites feed on insect eggs, while their larvae hitch a ride on other creatures, such as insects and spiders, and suck out their body fluids. Velvet mites live in soil and are very common. They get their name from the thick soft hair that covers the body.

Family	Trombidiidae
Number of species	At least 3,000
Length	⅙ in (4 mm)
Distribution	Worldwide

Velvet mite

Spiders

There are at least 40,000 species of spiders and all are hunters. Most prey on insects, but a few of the larger spiders catch small animals and birds. Spiders belong to a group called arachnids and they have four pairs of legs and no wings or antennae. Most have venom glands, but only a few are dangerous to humans.

Goliath bird-eating spider

Goliath bird-eating spider

This spider is strong enough to catch a bird, but it more often preys on frogs, small snakes, lizards, and insects. It pounces on its prey, seizing the creature with its strong legs and then paralyzes the victim with a poisonous bite. The spider cannot chew but it pours special digestive juices onto its prey that break down the body into liquid so the spider can suck the liquid up. If annoyed, this spider can make a hissing sound by rubbing its bristly legs together. It can also release tiny hairs from its body, which float through the air and cause serious irritation to any creature they happen to land on.

Family	Theraphosidae
Latin name	*Theraphosa blondi*
Length	Up to 12 in (30 cm)
Distribution	Northern South America

Funnel-web spiders

These spiders have an extremely poisonous bite that they use to kill prey, such as frogs and lizards as well as insects. The venom of one species—the Sydney funnel-web spider—is so powerful that it can even kill a human. These spiders also make a funnel-shaped web linked to an underground burrow. The spider hides in the burrow and if an insect walks across the web, the spider picks up the vibrations and rushes out to seize the prey.

Family	Dipluridae
Number of species	175
Length	Up to 5/8 in (1.5 cm)
Distribution	Subtropical and tropical areas worldwide

Funnel-web spider

Wolf spiders

These expert predators stalk their insect victims, then seize them with a final speedy pounce. Wolf spiders have much better eyesight than most spiders and this helps them find their prey. A couple of Australian species are even known to attack and kill the large and deadly cane toad.

Family	Lycosidae
Number of species	2,336
Length	Up to 1½ in (4 cm)
Distribution	Worldwide, except Arctic and Greenland

Wandering spiders

These aggressive venomous spiders often live on banana plants but also hunt insects on the ground. The most venomous species are those in the genus Phoneutria, which can be dangerous to humans.

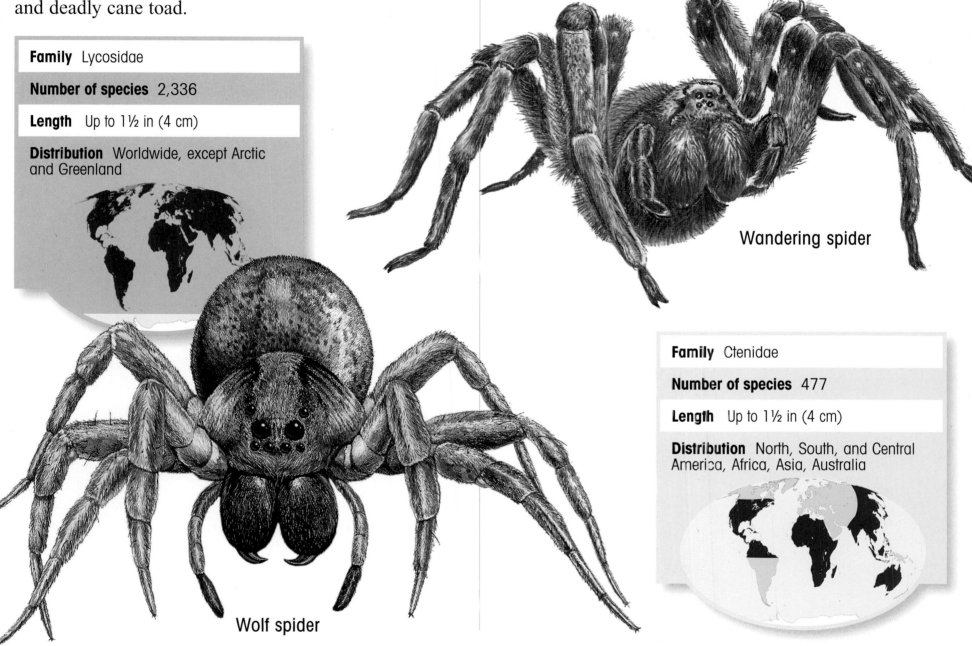

Wandering spider

Family	Ctenidae
Number of species	477
Length	Up to 1½ in (4 cm)
Distribution	North, South, and Central America, Africa, Asia, Australia

Wolf spider

Giant crab spiders

The long-legged crab spiders prey on insects and other invertebrates as well as small lizards, which they catch with their strong fangs. These spiders are often mottled in color, which helps them hide on tree bark. If threatened, the spider flattens itself against the bark so it is difficult to see.

Family	Sparassidae
Number of species	1,038
Length	Up to 1 in (2.5 cm)
Distribution	Worldwide, excluding Arctic

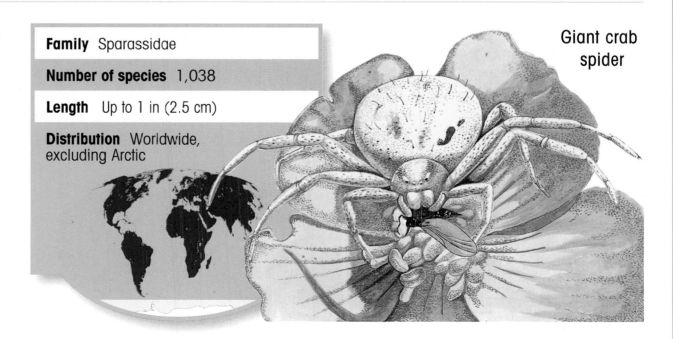

Giant crab spider

Spider traps

Not many killer creatures make traps for catching prey, but spiders have come up with an astonishing range of cunning devices. Many of these are made of silk, which the spider produces from small nozzlelike openings linked to special glands at the end of its body. A spider's silk is very thin but incredibly strong and there several kinds, which can be used for different purposes. Spiders use silk to make webs, line their burrows, and wrap up struggling prey so it cannot escape.

A silken web

The webs made by the orb weaver spider are a common sight—they can often be seen strung between plants or other supports. The spider can make two sorts of silk—sticky and non-sticky. It starts by spinning a non-sticky framework for its web and then adds more spokes and supports. Once these are all in place, the spider spins a sticky spiral at the center of the web that will trap its prey. The spider can then move around the outside of its web, keeping watch for prey without getting trapped itself. If prey flies into the web, the spider quickly bites it and wraps it in more silk. The sheet-web spider makes a slightly different kind of web, which looks a little like a flat silken hammock. The spider waits beneath for prey to fall into its trap.

The net-casting, or gladiator, spider has yet another kind of web. It makes a small square of sticky silk, which it holds with its four front legs. The spider hangs from a twig watching for prey and if something comes near, the spider stretches the net wide and quickly pops the web over the prey, trapping the creature underneath.

Above A golden orb weaver sits at the center of her web, while a jumping spider tries to avoid getting caught as it stalks the orb weaver's much smaller mate.

Hunting tactics

Other spiders make different kinds of traps. The spitting spider has a simple approach. It traps its victim with strands of a sticky substance that it spits out from special glands on its head. As it spits, the spider moves its head from side to side so that the strands fall in zigzags over the prey and pin the victim to the ground.

The trapdoor spider is an expert burrower and digs a tunnel in the ground. It lines the walls with a mixture of silk, earth, and saliva (spit) and then makes a flaplike door of silk at the top of the burrow. The spider then waits just inside this door until it senses the approach of prey. Quick as a flash, the spider springs out of its door, seizes the prey, and drags the creature down into its burrow.

Right A net-casting spider hangs from a support, with its sticky web held ready like a string bag to catch its prey.

The water spider

The water spider makes an amazing silken air chamber underwater. This is not a trap for prey, but a structure that allows the spider to live and hunt underwater. Once the spider has made its silken bell, it makes many journeys to the water's surface to collect bubbles of air with its legs. It then takes these down to the bell where they are trapped by the silk. Once the structure is filled with air, the spider can sit in its bell, breathing air and watching for prey, which it drags into the bell to eat.

Octopuses, sea stars, and worms

Octopuses and squid belong to the same group of invertebrates as snails and slugs—the mollusks. There are at least 100,000 species of mollusks and they have a wide range of body forms. Some live on land or in freshwater, but the majority live in the sea. Sea stars are echinoderms, a group of sea creatures that includes brittle stars, sea urchins, and sea cucumbers. There are many types of worms. Some remain in one place and filter food from the water. Others, such as paddle worms, hunt for their food.

Octopus

Octopus

The octopus usually hides during the day and hunts at night. It preys on other sea creatures, which it grabs with its tentacles. These are lined with powerful suckers, which help the octopus hold its prey. It swims by pulling itself along with its arms, or tentacles, and can also move by shooting jets of water out of its body to propel itself forward.

Longfin squid

This squid has a long body, eight arms, and two longer limbs called tentacles, which it can stretch out to grab prey. It moves fast by shooting water out of its body, which propels it along. It usually hunts at night and preys on fish, crustaceans, and other squid, which it catches with the help of the strong suckers on the underside of its arms at the

Family	Loliginidae
Latin name	*Loligo pealeii*
Length	Up to 20 in (50 cm)
Distribution	Western Atlantic

Family	Octopodidae
Latin name	*Octopus vulgaris*
Length	Up to 4½ ft (1.4 m)
Distribution	Temperate and tropical coastal waters

Longfin squid

Thorny sea star

This sea star has five thick arms, which are covered with short spines. On the underside of each arm are two rows of structures called tube feet. These work together, extending and contracting, to help the sea star move around. The sea star also uses its suckers to pull open the shells of prey, such as clams and oysters. Once the shell is open, the sea star can insert its stomach into the shell to digest the contents and then bring the stomach back into its body.

Family	Echinasteridae
Latin name	*Echinaster sentus*
Length	Up to 7 in diameter (18 cm)
Distribution	Western Atlantic, Caribbean Sea

Thorny sea star

Family	Ophiotrichidae
Latin name	*Ophiothrix fragilis*
Length	Body: ¾ in (2 cm)
Distribution	Eastern Atlantic, Mediterranean Sea

Brittle star

Brittle star

Like all brittle stars, this animal has a small body but its arms, which are covered in sharp spines, can be up to 4 in (10 cm) long. These arms are very delicate and break easily. Its mouth is on the underside of the body disk. The brittle star uses its long arms to catch small sea creatures and pass them to its mouth. It is also a scavenger and eats any rotting matter it comes across in the water.

Paddle worm

This large, sea-living worm has four pairs of sensory tentacles on its head and lots of tiny leaflike paddles down each side of its body. It preys mostly on other worms.

Paddle worm

Family	Phyllodocidae
Latin name	*Phyllodoce* sp.
Length	Up to 18 in (46 cm)
Distribution	Atlantic and Pacific coasts of North America

Crabs, lobsters, and jellyfish

Crabs and lobsters both belong to a group of invertebrates called crustaceans, which also includes barnacles and shrimp. There are about 40,000 species, most of which live in the sea or in freshwater. All larger crustaceans live by hunting other creatures. Jellyfish and sea anemones are part of a group known as cnidarians. A typical cnidarian has a tubelike body with a central mouth, surrounded by tentacles bearing stinging cells. Most cnidarians live in the sea, although some are found in freshwater.

Atlantic lobster

Atlantic lobster

The lobster lives mostly in rocky-bottomed waters where it crawls over the seabed searching for food. It attacks its prey with the large pincers on its front legs, crushing hard shells with the larger part of the pincers. It then tears the flesh with the smaller sections, which are equipped with sharp teeth. Lobsters are not fussy about their prey and feed on crabs, mussels, clams, fish, and worms. They will also eat dead creatures if they come across them.

Family Nephropidae

Latin name *Homarus americanus*

Length 24–34 in (61–86 cm)

Distribution Atlantic coast of North America

Blue crab

Like most crabs, the blue crab has a hard shell and five pairs of legs. The front pair is equipped with pincers for catching and holding prey. The shell is twice as wide as it is long. These crabs swim and crawl and are very active. They usually hunt during the day—oysters and clams are blue crabs favorite prey.

Family Portunidae

Latin name *Callinectes sapidus*

Length 10 in (25 cm)

Distribution Western Atlantic; introduced into Eastern Atlantic and Japan

Blue crab

Portuguese man-of-war

Although it is a cnidarian, the Portuguese man-of-war is not a jellyfish but a siphonophore. And it is not one creature but a colony of lots of organisms, some of which catch prey, while others digest food or lay eggs. The float, which sits on the water's surface, is quite small but the tentacles can be up to 165 ft (50 m) long. They are covered with stinging cells, which are used to kill or paralyze fish and other prey.

Family Physaliidae

Latin name *Physalia physalis*

Length Float: 12 in (30 cm)

Distribution Warm areas of Atlantic, Pacific, and Indian oceans

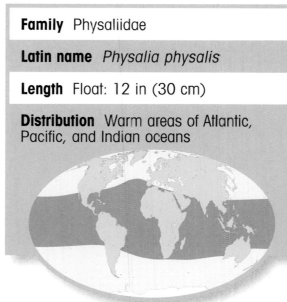

Portuguese man-of-war

Purple jellyfish

The tentacles of this jellyfish may grow to up to 10 ft (3 m) long and are covered with tiny stinging cells. The jellyfish uses these to defend itself against attackers and to kill prey, such as smaller jellyfish and other tiny sea creatures.

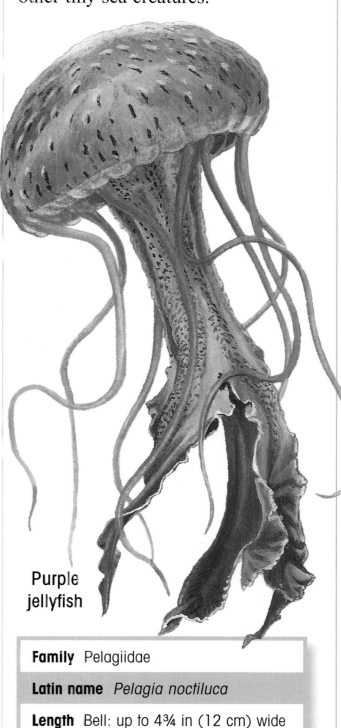

Purple jellyfish

Family Pelagiidae

Latin name *Pelagia noctiluca*

Length Bell: up to 4¾ in (12 cm) wide

Distribution Warm areas of Atlantic, Pacific, and Indian oceans

Family Actiniidae

Latin name *Cribrinopsis albopunctata*

Length 6 in (15 cm)

Distribution Pacific coast of North America

Strawberry anemone

This anemone has a sucking disk at the base of its body. This keeps the anemone attached to a rock or other surface in the sea. Its mouth is at the center of the body and is surrounded by stinging tentacles. If anything touches these tentacles, the stinging cells are fired off, paralyzing the victim, which the anemone then pushes into its mouth.

Strawberry anemone

Glossary

Amphibian
Typically, a four-legged vertebrate animal that can live on land and in water and usually lays eggs in water. Frogs and toads are amphibians.

Antarctica
The continent around the South Pole.

Arctic
The region around the North Pole.

Barbel
A whiskery structure near the nose and mouth of some fish. It is used to help the fish taste and feel as it searches for food.

Camouflage
The colors or patterns on an animal's body that help it blend in with its surroundings so it cannot easily be seen by enemies or prey.

Carnivorous
A carnivorous animal is one that feeds on flesh. In strict zoological terms, a carnivore is a member of the order Carnivora, which includes cats, dogs, and bears.

Carrion
The bodies of animals that have died of natural causes or been killed by other animals.

Clutch
A set of eggs produced and incubated at one time.

Cold-blooded
Used to describe reptiles and amphibians that cannot control their own body temperature but must rely on the heat of the sun for warmth.

Colony
A group of individuals of a single species living together in one place. Ants, termites, and some bees and wasps live in colonies.

Constriction
A method of killing prey used by some snakes. The snake wraps its body around the prey and squeezes so that the animal cannot breathe.

Crest
A structure on top of an animal's head, usually made of bone or skin, used by males in displays to warn off other males or to attract females.

Echolocation
Bats and whales use echolocation to help them find prey. The animal makes a high-pitched sound and uses the echoes that bounce off any object in its path to work out the size and position of that object.

Endangered
Describes animals that are very rare and in danger of becoming extinct.

Extinct
Describes a species of animal that is no longer in existence.

Family
A group of related genera, which are themselves groups of related species. The scientific name of a family usually ends in -idae.

Fang
Large pointed tooth, sometimes used to inject venom into prey.

Fertilization
The joining of an egg cell with sperm to create a new cell. Fertilization can happen inside or outside of the female's body.

Gill
A respiratory organ used by aquatic animals for breathing the oxygen in water.

Gland
A part of the body that produces special substances, such as poisons, which are passed to the outside of the body. Some snakes have glands that produce venom.

Habitat
The surroundings in which an animal lives, including the climate, water, and plant life.

Hibernation
The process of going into a deep sleep or dormant state during the winter. A hibernating animal's body temperature and heart rate drop to save energy.

Incubation

Keeping eggs warm with the parent's body or with soil or other coverings.

Insect

Small air-breathing invertebrates belonging to the class Insecta, with bodies divided into three parts (head, thorax, and abdomen). They have three pairs of legs and usually two pairs of wings.

Invertebrate

An animal without a backbone. Insects and spiders, as well as creatures, such as slugs, snails, crabs, and clams, are invertebrates.

Larva

A young form of a creature, which hatches from an egg. A larva looks different from the adult. A tadpole, for example, is the larva of a frog.

Mammal

A warm-blooded animal, usually four-legged and hairy, which gives birth to fully formed young. Female mammals feed their young on milk from their mammary glands.

Mating

The coming together of a male and female creature to produce young.

Migration

The regular movement of groups of animals from one region to another for feeding or breeding.

Mollusk

A type of invertebrate animal, such as a snail, slug, or clam. Many, but not all, mollusks have hard shells.

Order

A group of related families.

Predator

A creature that hunts and kills other creatures for food.

Prehensile

Describes a part of the body, such as a tail, that can grasp things. Some snakes have a prehensile tail, which they can use like a fifth limb to hold on to branches.

Prey

Animals that are hunted and eaten by other animals.

Rain forest

Forested area near the equator, which is hotter and wetter than any other forests.

Reptile

A vertebrate animal with scaly skin that lays eggs with tough, leathery shells. Dinosaurs were reptiles. Modern reptiles include tortoises, snakes, lizards, and crocodiles.

Rodent

An animal in the mammal group Rodentia, which includes rats, mice, and squirrels.

Scavenger

A creature that feeds on the remains of dead animals.

School

A group of fish that travels together.

Skeleton

The bony supporting structure of an animal's body.

Spawn

To deposit eggs directly into the water, as fish and amphibians do.

Species

A type of animal. Living things of the same species can mate and produce young.

Swim bladder

A gas-filled sac in the body of a fish that helps it float.

Territory

The area where a mammal normally lives and feeds. Some animals defend their territory fiercely.

Venom

A liquid made by snakes or other animals that is used to kill or paralyze prey.

Vertebrate

An animal with a backbone. Mammals, birds, reptiles, amphibians, and fish are all vertebrates.

Index

Index

Acknowledgments

Illustrators

Graham Allen, Alan Male, Colin Newman, Dick Twinney

Marshall Editions would like to thank the following for their kind permission to reproduce their images:

b = bottom   **c** = center   **t** = top   **l** = left   **r** = right

All images inside of this book (except pages 117 and 128–129) are reproduced courtesy of FLPA and its associate agencies.

Pages: 1 Frans Lanting; **2–3** Sergey Gorshkov/Minden Pictures; **4–5** Ingo Arndt/Minden Pictures; **6–7** Vivek Sharma/Minden Pictures; **7b** Nigel Cattlin; **10–11** Vivek Sharma/Minden Pictures; **24t** Christian Ziegler/Minden Pictures; **24–25, 34, 34c** ImageBroker; **35t** Otto Plantema/Minden Pictures; **34–35** Cyril Ruoso/Minden Pictures; **40b** Minden Pictures; **41t** Thomas Mangelsen/Minden Pictures; **40–41** Suzi Eszterhas/Minden Pictures; **48t** Frans Lanting; **48b** Peter Davey; **49** Frans Lanting; **50–51** Richard Costin; **68** Sunset; **69t** Fritz Polking; **69b** Stephen Dalton/NHPA; **74t** Neil Bowman; **74b** Stephen Dalton/NHPA; **75** Koos Delport; **76–77** Pete Oxford/Minden Pictures; **80l** Fritz Polking; **81r** Konrad Wothe/Minden Pictures; **80–81** Yva Momatiuk & John Eastcott; **84t** Kevin Schafer/Minden Pictures; **85t** Winfried Schaefer/ImageBroker; **84–85** Thomas Marent/Minden Pictures; **100–101** Albert Visage; **108t** Flip Nicklin/Minden Pictures; **109t** Chris Mattison; **108–109** Piotr Naskrecki/Minden Pictures; **116b** Marcel van Kammen/Minden Pictures; **116t** Marcel van Kammen/Minden Pictures; **117** Shutterstock/Holly Kuchera; **122–123** Norbert Wu/Minden Pictures; **123br** Norbert Wu/Minden Pictures; **128–129** Mark Bowler; **129br** Chris Newbert/Minden Pictures; **130–131** Mark Moffett/Minden Pictures; **136** S & D & K Maslowski; **137tr** Erica Olsen; **137b** ImageBroker; **137bc** FotoNatura/Minden; **142bl** Nigel Cattlin; **143tr** Roger Tidman; **142–143** Michael & Patricia Fogden/Minden Pictures; **148–149** Michael Weber/Image Broker; **149t** Piotr Naskrecki/Minden Pictures; **149b** Silvestris Fotoservice